THE INVESTING BIBLE

Table of Contents

REAL ESTATE INVESTING 101

THE DIVIDEND INVESTING BLUEPRINT

REAL ESTATE INVESTING 101

BY

CHAD MALONE

INTRODUCTION

Like many people out there, you're probably looking for that one financial solution that ends all your money problems and frustration, am I right?

Of course, I am! But we know that making money outside of a job is a daunting task and a headache for most.

Coming up with an idea of what to do can be one of the hardest parts of starting up a business, and let's face it, we've got a very slim chance of starting the next Facebook or Uber.

So here we are. It's the property game, one of the most lucrative, sustainable business models out there that have made the most millionaires in history and also one of the very few that have the best blueprint to follow with regard to creating wealth in a step by step format.

I know it's scary. It was very scary for me too, especially at the beginning. But aren't all kinds of business? Especially if you don't have previous experience or education relevant to this industry.

This is normal especially due to the fact that while real estate investment can be an extremely lucrative business no matter how old you are, it normally requires lots of time commitment and of course, a huge amount of money — or extremely good credit — just to get started. If you happen to be a busy millennial with not a lot of cash to spare, then a real estate investment trust or REIT might be a good place for you to start. But there are also many other alternatives.

Now, let's go back to the most important question to answer when investing in real estate… *can you afford it?*

I said "the most important" because it's an expensive endeavour to dive into, so looking into your budget should be a priority. Unless you have a lot of money laying around, you'll probably need to take alternative options for getting started with your investment. Investing in real estate is definitely a serious commitment, and your financial capability controls your ability to run this business.

Another question that you need to answer is... why?

You have to really understand your purpose as to why you want to invest in the real estate business. If you're investing to meet the needs of your family, then it would be smart to look at the land's papers and formalities like electricity, water, and the road connectivity to the estate. The location's proximity to shops, schools, and other establishments are some of the other things you must consider. If you're investing in a house that you're planning to turn into a home, then you must put a great consideration to the home's interior to see the extent of repairs that are necessary to make it comfortable to live in for you and your family.

If you're buying the estate exclusively for the purpose of reselling later on, then you must do more research on your choice of investment. You need to be aware of how much of an appreciation the land goes through and also analyse which areas are the ones that are going to bring you a return on investment. This is important as you don't want to put all your investment money on something that may not sell.

These points are only two of the important things you must consider when you want to invest in real estate – there are other important things you must know to be successful at it.

In this book, I'm going to give you a walkthrough on everything you need to know when investing in real estate and how to go about it to attain success in it.

Chapter 1

WHY INVEST IN REAL ESTATE?

The idea might just randomly come into your mind, or perhaps it's something that has always been bugging your mind. It might be a thoughtful little passing fantasy about purchasing that small seemingly abandoned house down the road and renovating it to sell for a profit. Or perhaps, you have considered buying a rental property and get rent to cover the mortgage. Regardless of how the idea formed in your mind, the important thing is that you've taken the step to learn how the world of real estate investment works.

Now, you know your personal reason... but the question is that, why is it a good idea?

The answer is that there is exceptional potential for revenue in real estate investment.

Investing in real estate is a sure-fire way of generating money and boosting your net worth. The money you make will likely depend on your knowledge, dedication, and game plan. There's no magic formula when it comes to real estate investment. Regardless of how simple the late-night millionaire's club makes this business seem, it wouldn't make you get rich overnight. It may take months and months before you can even buy a property, then more before you can sell one, and long before you can get a steady, comfortable revenue.

So, with the long process involved in this business, is it really worth it?

To put it simply, this IS a career option with potential revenue whose only real restrictions are those you put on yourself - and that is how you must treat it. It means that how much money you make entirely depends on you. You are your own boss. You have total control over your profits by being knowledgeable about investing and real estate, as well as being familiar with foreclosure laws and loan structures, understanding the psychology behind selling and buying, and learning your rules and responsibilities as an owner or seller.

As long as you know what you're really doing, it can almost guarantee you can make money. Unlike a lot of other investments, you are able to depend on one thing with real estate. You are able to eventually make a profit on almost any kind of property you have – on the condition that you paid a practical amount for it in the first place. The value of real estate goes up and down depending on the economy. When real estate prices go down, it's inevitable for them to go back up again.

If you have decided to invest in rental properties, then expect to have a steady flow of income – as long as you're making sure that they are well-maintained. Here's one universal truth about real estate: housing will always be in demand. People will always need it – after all, shelter is at the first level of Maslow's hierarchy of needs. And even in the most challenging markets, rental prices rarely drop much. If you are able to keep your rental units filled with good tenants who pay on time, you can rely on the income from those units to settle mortgage and maintenance expenses to eventually generate profit.

So, the bottom line here is that real estate is a form of investment that takes many years but is a sure way to generate profits. Only if you ignore all the "be a millionaire overnight" promises and false publicity, you will find the real truth: investing in real estate is one of the best ways to be financially stable. And that, after all, is the best reason why you should consider investing in real estate.

1.1 Why It's the Best Vehicle to Reach Financial Freedom

Is it your goal to be rich? Now, you probably think that real estate could be the answer to make this happen. Even though this might be partially true, money isn't necessarily the major benefit of pursuing real estate investment. Personally, I think that the main reward of pushing through this endeavour is to finally live your life just the way you want to. In this sub-chapter, let's dig deeper into how real estate investment can eventually help you reach that form of freedom.

Do you work hard at the moment? Do you think you're not living your life now due to the time and dedication you put in your current work? With the amount of work you're probably dealing with at the moment, do you still have time to spend with your friends and family? I'm pretty sure that you can hardly do that with the time you need to spend at work.

Now, ask yourself… Is it really worth it? Is that really the only way for you to make money?

Fortunately, I realized early in life that working too much during your best years just to reach your goal is not worth it if you're sacrificing the time you could have spent with your family and other people important to you, doing the things that you couldn't do when you're old and ill. If you're starting to feel that life is simply passing you by, then reconsider your decisions, and consider finding a new way to earn a living.

At some point in your life, you may come to the realization that working to afford what you need and want is actually obstructing you from reaching happiness and satisfaction. The stress you get from your workplace, the demands thrown at you by your condescending boss, and juggling all of these with social and family life can be pretty overwhelming to the point that life seems to be pushing you in the pit of misery. This could be quite a push to come to a decision to finally leave the life of a rat race and work toward financial freedom.

Investing in real estate is definitely one of the best ways you can opt for to escape the rat race and earn a living without having to sacrifice other important moments and people of your life. Real estate investment makes a lot of sense when you want to have enough money to support your and your family's needs without stressing too much about working.

With the help of profitable rental properties, you are able to have income even if you decide to quit your current full-time job. But before signing any resignation form, it's extremely important to make yourself knowledgeable about the right steps you need to take in order to build your own portfolio of assets that are going to serve as your source of income.

Money is very important to many people, while there are still some who might argue that happiness is more important. But do you really have to choose just one? Personally, I'd have both of them as much as possible. And yes, it's pretty achievable! So, I urge you to try to live your life how you want it to be, and one of the ways to do that is to invest in real estate.

1.2 Depreciation vs Appreciation

You've probably heard of these terms before aside from real estate; these terms also relate to the value of the currency, stocks, and bonds. However, in the world of real estate, appreciation and depreciation have a little different meaning. Okay, so basically, depreciation is when the value of a property goes down, and appreciation is when the value of a property goes up.

1.2.1 Why Appreciation and Depreciation Happen?

Appreciation may occur when there are changes in the supply and demand of a product or service. When the supply go up and the demand goes down, that's when depreciation comes into the picture.

Here are the most common reasons that lead to depreciation:

- ❖ A massive decline in the market

- ❖ Leaving the property unmaintained

- ❖ Changes in the local neighbourhood

On the other hand, things that can lead to appreciation include:

- ❖ Developments in the nearby areas

- ❖ Home expansion and general improvement

- ❖ Road improvements

The changes in the value of an asset can vary significantly over time. Other assets, which are also known as long-term assets, may lose or gain more value gradually over time.

1.3 Equity Explained

Equity is another term you need to understand when you're getting into real estate investment. Basically, equity is the difference between the property's market value and the money that is owed to the lender. The equity is the money you would get when the mortgage is paid off if you decide to sell the property.

Okay, let me give you a simple example to make it easier for you to understand: Let's say the market value of your property is $300,000 and you owe $200,000 for the mortgage. Your equity then is $100,000 if you happen to sell the property at fair market value.

"Net" Equity

On the other hand, what we call as net equity is different from gross equity. It is your gross equity minus the expenses spent in selling the property. These costs might include the commissions for the realtor, unpaid property taxes, and any closing expenses you have to settle.

Okay, let's give you another example. Let's say the property amounts to $300,000, and it has $200,000 mortgage; then it is going to have $100,000 as equity. But there's a BUT – you owe a commission of $15,000 to your realtor. But keep in mind that you also have to settle the closing expenses like title charges, escrow fees, and tax proration, which may add somewhere around $5,000 in seller-paid expenses. Now, subtract those numbers from your equity.

All in all, net equity is the amount you'd actually keep when the deal is closed.

1.3.1 Building Home Equity

There are many different ways in which homeowners can build home equity. The amount of down payment you put on a property makes the initial mortgage much lower. For instance, if you put in 30% down payment on a property that is valued at $100,000, then you'd start with an equity of $30,000 even before making a mortgage payment. Then the remaining $70,000 would be the mortgage.

Pay Attention to the Mortgage Payment

With every mortgage payment you make, you are building equity. Each payment you make creates a difference in the principal balance that you owe. Every payment also comes with interest on the loan and normally property tax and insurance premium payments too. As you slowly settle mortgage payments and you are able to make extra payments to apply to the principal, your equity goes up.

When Making Home Improvements

Your equity goes up if you make home improvements that upsurge your property's fair market value. For instance, you might have to spend $40,000 to remodel a part of the house, which makes the market value of the property go up by $20,000. Now you have increased your equity by $20,000, assuming you did not take out a home equity loan to afford that new kitchen.

Comparable Sales

Your property's fair market value can go up because the other houses in your area are currently selling for a higher amount. You may have purchased your home a couple of years ago for $150,000 and laid out 20% down payment for it. The same homes are now selling for about $180,000. Your equity in the home has gone up by $30,000 because of this increase.

This rise is also hypothetical. You must sell the home in order to realize this equity. But then again, it's going to be reflected in an appraisal.

1.3.2 How to Reduce Home Equity?

You could also see your home equity go down. Values went down in almost every real estate market in the country in the past few years. When the value of housing falls, equity goes down with it. Your equity goes down if homes sell for less in your area, mainly when you are underwater on your mortgage or on the edge of it.

You might have purchased a home for $300,000 with 20% down payment, which is $60,000. But then, the real estate market went down, and now the same properties are selling for $200,000. Your property value has gone down by $100,000, so you no longer have any equity in the property. If you sold your property for $200,000, you would need to pay out of pocket in order to pay the mortgage lender to settle the difference.

You could also reduce your equity by increasing the principal loans on the property. If you refinance your mortgage or take another mortgage or home equity loan, you will most likely reduce your equity.

If the property burns down or is otherwise ruined in a natural disaster and you happen to not have enough insurance coverage to make up for the loss, then it just means that you have lost your home as well as your equity.

The expenses needed to fix the problems will use up your equity position if you do not consistently make repairs to the home as things decline or stop working properly.

By the end of the deal, you'll find out the equity that comes with the property. If you are able to negotiate a better selling price, you will increase the equity in the deal. And if you happen to not pay for repairs as requested by the purchaser or give the buyer credit for closing expenses, your equity will go up.

1.4 Difference between Assets and Liabilities

Whether you are an accounting expert or not, it's extremely important for you to know the basics of assets and liabilities. Being able to know the difference between the two financial accounts might make all the difference between becoming rich or becoming poor. Now, in this sub-chapter, I want to dig deep into the difference between these two accounts and to offer you some basic knowledge that even laypersons will understand.

1.4.1 Assets Explained

Assets are anything that could be owned by a person or business and that carry a positive cash value. In other words, assets produce income. Here are some examples of assets: real estate, investment, and businesses – all of these can generate income. Assets are things that will give you return on investment.

Now, there are three classes that assets could be categorized under. These are current assets, fixed assets, and intangible assets. By being aware of the difference between these 3 classifications, you can easily understand how to record revenue on financial statements.

Current assets are cash-on-hand or assets that you can turn into cash within a short period of time. Current assets fund daily operations. Companies make use of current assets in order to run their daily operations as this is better than using the money on interest from short-term financing. There are 5 accounts listed under current assets. These accounts include investments, cash, accounts receivable, prepaid expenses and inventory.

Fixed assets are known to be tangible property. Fixed assets cannot be easily turned into cash, unlike current assets. Some of the examples of fixed assets are machines and equipment, property, and buildings. This may also include computers. Fixed assets get special tax treatment and could also be denigrated.

Intangible assets are the items that can't be touched physically. These items could be turned into cash, but they normally hold value to the individual or business that represent it. Some of the examples of intangible assets include trademarks, patents, and copyrights. You will have two different types of intangible assets that are known as the legal intangibles and competitive intangibles. It is recommended that you see your accountant for further advice on intangible assets too.

1.4.2 Liabilities Explained

Now that the assets are clearer to you, let's talk about their evil twin – liabilities. Liabilities are anything that's owned by a person or business that have to be repaid. Unlike assets, liabilities do not generate money, but instead, costs us money. Liabilities are debts that should be repaid back and normally with interest.

There are two categories of liabilities. The first one is the current liabilities, and the other one is long-term liabilities. Both of these classes of liabilities have to be paid back and are counted as debt.

Current liabilities are considered debt that should be paid back within a period of one year. This debt normally is repaid through the current assets account, then again, this is not always the case. There are a lot of different categories of current liabilities. They include accounts payable, notes payable, dividends payable, and short-term debt.

Now that I have explained the differences between assets and liabilities, it has to be stated that it's in the best interest of both the individual and business to have a lot more assets and fewer liabilities. This is how you become wealthy, as you try to not get too many liabilities, particularly if the assets that generate income cannot afford them.

What other people usually invest in and why real estate is the best option for stability because of capital growth.

Where to invest money is a question that has no fixed answer as it changes constantly with time. By investing your money safely, you earn next to nothing. On the other hand, by investing your money in a riskier asset, trouble is almost always inevitable. So, the question is where do people invest and why real estate could be the best way to go.

In more than 20 years of investing money, I have never found the question of *"where to invest your money"* harder than it is now. It is a whole new scenario where interest rates are very low in a weak or ever-changing economy. Now, let's make the best of it and check out the alternatives.

For most investors, the answer to this question begins with mutual funds; it's the investment of choice providing a lot of possibilities. Let's begin at the safest funds being offered.

Money funds place your money in safe money market securities and then pay interest in the form of dividends that go up when interest rates rise and go down when rates decrease. They currently pay returns that are close to zero after expenses, emulating the condition of the current money market. Eventually, interest rates will go up and then money funds might look better.

In the meantime, check out the tax-free versions that pay interest that's free from federal income tax. Whether you believe it or not, a lot of them are paying a higher bonus yield than their taxable counterparts.

Bond funds have been the common answer to where to invest your money in order to earn more interest income. That is good news. On the other hand, the bad news is that, when it comes to investing money and changes in interest rates, they are the opposite of money funds. Bond funds do not get more attractive as interest rates increase. Instead, they lose money, and so do their investors.

1.5 Some of the Most Popular Investment Options Today

Stocks

Stocks are risky and need a lot of research. However, even though this is the case, stocks may offer highly rewarding ROI.

Cryptocurrency

After Bitcoin suddenly overtook the market, people started investing in it, and more cryptocurrencies came out in the market. The problem about this, however, is that the value of it may change rapidly and drastically.

Money Market Funds and Accounts

Money market funds and accounts are popular options because of their extremely low risk. Money market funds invest in low risk and liquid securities like cash equivalent securities, cash, and US Treasury.

Savings Accounts

Savings accounts are also considered very safe and most liquid investment next to cash. They pay very low interest – averagely just a little over 2% as of 2019.

Despite the popularity of different options mentioned above, investing in the real estate market remains one of the best options.

Real estate investment is the purchase of a future income stream from a property and could offer a lot of advantages over other types of investments, which include potentially higher returns, inflation hedging, stability, and variation.

1.5.1 Investing at a Young Age

Investing while you're young is a habit that we, as a society, have to teach the youth. It's not enough that we let the youth find it out themselves. We have to provide the youngsters with formal education not just about the importance of investing at a young age but also about the way they can do it wisely.

What are the benefits of investing at a young age?

First of all, investing at a young age helps you get your much-needed head start, which is very important in maximizing the benefit of letting investments grow over time. If you start to invest early, you get more time in your life to let your investments grow; this is due to the benefits of compound interest and letting your investments increase and grow in value.

Another benefit of investing at an early age is that it gives you more time to recover from any mistakes. If you happen to end up losing some of the money you saved in the market, you'll be able to have more time to recover before actually needing the money if you're planning to invest on a long-term basis.

Furthermore, investing while you're young gives you the flexibility to make riskier investments. In case you lose a great amount of money at a young age, you'll have a lot of time ahead of you to recover from your losses and start again. On the other hand, if you choose to invest while you are a little bit older, then you might be much less risk-averse because you are not able to afford losing money, and you wouldn't have a lot of time on your side to recoup from the losses, before you need to take the money out of the market.

On top of that, you have to keep in mind that investing is a learning process. This means that investing while you're young will give you more time to learn from your mistakes and to set realistic goals that you know you can achieve later in life. Investing at a young age, if done properly, might mean that you'll have a better quality of life as you grow old. By failing to invest properly in your youth, the quality of your life might actually become worse in later years because you'll not have built up your future retirement funds appropriately.

Chapter 2

GETTING STARTED WITH OR WITHOUT MONEY

A lot of people believe that investing in real estate requires a lot of money.

But the truth is, this is still possible with little to no money at all! With many sources of funds available today, real estate investing has become accessible to people of any walk of life.

As opposed to many people's belief, the amount of money you invest will not make or break the deal you are going to do. It is a mistake to stop yourself from diving into the real estate world. Here are different ways you can invest in a real estate business with little to no money.

❖ Borrow the Money

This is possibly the easiest way to buy a property without making a down payment out of your pocket. You can either search for a lender that offers a low-interest rate or make use of a home equity or other type of credit loan that will still provide you with the tax benefits of a normal mortgage. You could also borrow funds from a real estate broker – arrange to borrow the commission of broker for a short period of time and use the funds as the down payment.

❖ Seller Financing

Another way to get started with real estate investment without making a down payment is with the help of the seller himself. If ever a seller refuses your down payment, you can ask if you can just pay higher monthly payments instead. There are also cases when the seller would be willing to pay for the down payment just to sell the house faster.

❖ Rent to Own

A lot of investors have no idea that they may be able to rent a property from the owner and eventually have the opportunity to purchase it. Depending on the terms of the lease agreement, of course, the buyer and seller can negotiate the total amount to be paid at the time agreed for living in the property. With this agreement, the renter will be able to buy the property at a certain price in a specific timeframe. Normally, the rental payments – might be partial or all – are going to be credited toward the total purchase price of the property.

❖ Use Your Valuable Personal Property

If you own anything valuable, you can use it as a down payment as a substitute for money. Do you have anything that you believe is more valuable than the price of the down payment? Some of the things you can use in replacement to cash are vehicles, jewellery, campers, boats, gadgets, appliances, and furniture.

❖ Shoulder the Seller's Debts

If you find a seller who is in need of cash to pay off other debts, you can offer to shoulder those debts rather than making a down payment.

❖ Find a Partner

This is another way to purchase a property without a down payment – search for other cash buyers. But then again, you have to be very careful with this one as this could be quite messy. So, how this works is you may organize the deal on a smaller scale by bringing in a person or two. In exchange for the financing, you can promise to take the responsibilities of setting up the deal and dealing with the real estate investment. This is something you can also do with the seller himself.

❖ Set Irresistible Offers

There are owners who might be willing to accept a higher price for the property, even though it means you have to pay with instalment, in lieu of accepting a down payment.

❖ Try Wholesaling

Let's say a wholesaler finds a property that is below market value. A wholesaler would acquire that property under contract with the seller and then assign or sell that contract to another buyer or investor, and that investor or buyer would complete the transaction with the seller. The wholesaler is not required to make any improvement on the property at all. The only responsibility is to get it under contract and sell the contract to another investor that's looking for a worn-down house that requires repair.

❖ Combine Mortgages

If you happen to have an existing property, you can combine mortgages in order to pay the seller with cash at closing without making use of your own money. You may also suggest that the seller place a second mortgage on the first and keep the cash, while you, on the other hand, shoulder both loans.

❖ Turn Your House into a Multi-rental

Also known as house hacking, multi-rental is a free way to start up a real estate business. And not only you can make money out of it, but you can also live in it for free! Okay, so the idea behind it is simple… you purchase a multifamily property (2 to 4 units), move into any of these units, and rent out the other units to others. Your tenants will be the ones to cover and pay off the mortgage and other house expenses.

Do your Research

There are specific sellers that might be more willing to accept no money down offers on a property than others. If the property has been available on the market for a long time or is advertised as a must sell, then the seller might be more than willing to agree with your offer. On top of this, just like any other real estate investment, make sure to do research on it beforehand.

2.1 What Are Carrying Costs on a Real Estate Investment

To put it simply, real estate carrying costs are the costs you sustain by reason of your ownership of a specific piece of property. There are properties that are "cash-flow positive," and there are also some that are "cash-flow negative", which means that some properties earn more money in comparison to what they actually cost in order to maintain and some earn less than the "carrying costs". The ones that earn less are normally acquired by the owner for residential or recreational purposes. Some investment properties could be cash-flow negative if one can fairly predict that the resale value of the property will go up to an extent that will recover the negative cash-flow throughout the period of ownership and, presumably some profit as well.

The standard real estate carrying costs include:

- ❖ Homeowners' association (HOA) dues

- ❖ Insurance

- ❖ Maintenance

- ❖ Property taxes

- ❖ Your mortgage payments

However, there are also some investors who consider marketing expenses as holding costs if they are done on a recurring basis. There are different carrying costs for different types of investors: fix and flippers and buy-and-hold investors.

2.1.1 Real Estate Carrying Costs for Fix and Flippers

A fix-and-flip investor buys a property with the plan of renovating it and selling it for a profit. The real estate holding costs are the expenses connected with keeping the property before selling it. These carrying costs always depend on the fix and flipper's budget. They must know how much the carrying costs are going to be, so they know how much it will cost to flip a property.

Fix-and-flip carrying costs normally consist of:

- ❖ Property taxes

- ❖ Property insurance

- ❖ Mortgage payment

- ❖ Utilities

- ❖ HOA fees

- ❖ Marketing fees

Remember that acquisition costs, rehab costs, and real estate agent fees aren't normally considered carrying costs since they are one-time payments and not accrued on a recurring basis.

2.1.2 Real Estate Carrying Costs for Buy-and-Hold Investors

Buy and hold real estate is a long-term investment method. This is where an investor buys a property and keeps or holds onto it for as long as he wants. This investor may have the intention of selling it eventually or rent it out to cover the money spent to own it.

Buy-and-hold investment property carrying costs include:

- ❖ Property taxes

- ❖ Rental property insurance

- ❖ Mortgage payment

- ❖ Utilities

- ❖ Maintenance

- ❖ HOA Fees

- ❖ Property management fees

- ❖ Marketing fees

2.1.3 Examples of Real Estate Carrying Costs

Check out some of the examples of carrying costs and how they affect your ROI.

Let's assume the following costs on a fix-and-flip project:

Acquisition Costs

Down payment: $30,000

Closing costs: $15,000

Mortgage amount: $150,000

Total Acquisition Costs: $195,000

Monthly Carrying Costs

Mortgage payment: $1,000

Property taxes: $300

Property insurance: $100

Utilities: $100

HOA fees: $100

Marketing fees: $150

Total Monthly Carrying Costs: $1,950

Now, let's say that it takes you about 3 months to fix and sell the property; your rehab and other expenses to sell the property are $25,000, and you sell the property for $300,000.

The total investment is the carrying costs multiplied by 3 then add the acquisition costs, rehab, and sales expenses.

$1,950 x 3 = $5,850

$5,850 + $195,000 + $30,000 = $230,850, which then becomes your total investment.

In order to know your ROI, you just have to divide your profit by the investment's total amount then multiply it by 100.

Your total profit is the sales price minus the total amount of your investment

$300,000 – $230,850= $69,150 profit

$69,150/$230,850=0.30x100=30%ROI

The calculation above shows the profit from one deal, which is generally how fix and flippers do calculation of their ROI on a per property basis.

Based on this example, you can calculate the total monthly carrying costs to help you calculate the budget you need to get into the real estate investment business. They also heavily influence your ROI. The shorter your timeline is and the lower your carrying costs are, the higher your ROI will be, all other things being equal.

2.2 Tips on Dealing with Real Estate Carrying Costs

Dealing and managing the carrying cost is one of the top responsibilities of a real estate investor. This is very important because by overlooking this, you can potentially go over the specified budget. This can cause a decrease in ROI.

But then again, if you are well aware of your carrying costs upfront, you are able to account for them, plan consequently, and don't get out of your budget. Here are important things you have to do to control the real estate carrying costs:

❖ **Be Aware of the Real Estate Holding Expenses Upfront**

As an investor, you have to understand your real estate carrying costs right before signing any contract. By doing this, you will know if you can afford the property, what are the total costs to own the property, and how much the rent should be.

❖ **Keep Your Eyes on the Rehab Supplies**

Rehab supplies influence the total carrying costs. Vacant property has higher theft compared to an occupied one. The occurrences of theft could increase the carrying costs and at the same time, lower the ROI.

❖ **Add the Renovation Expenses to the Total Expenses**

Renovations affect the real estate holding expenses by a great deal. Most of the time, investors overlook the additional financing and utility expenses once the renovations run over the specified timeline.

2.3 Top Options to Finance Your Investment with Limited Funds

While these methods were mentioned in our previous list, let's go deeper into these two options as I think these are two of the options I would always recommend.

2.3.1 Lease Option Agreement

This home buying option can be used when buyers are engaged in credit repair but are not able to qualify for bank financing. Basically, lease options are a layaway plan that lets the buyers settle the payment through monthly instalments for a prearranged amount of time.

A lease-purchase option agreement could be planned to meet the needs of both parties but should stand by state laws. Most sellers need a down payment in order to secure the property for sale and pay a portion of monthly rental payments toward the purchase of the property.

Lease option contracts should be prepared by an estate lawyer. This form of contract applies different rules depending on the state and might involve a lease option to buy, purchase agreement, or lease option.

Types of Lease Purchase Option Agreements

Lease options are the most commonly used contract for rent-to-own properties. Buyers need to offer 'options' money in order to secure the home that is being purchased. The main setback of using option money, however, is that funds are non-refundable and don't apply toward the purchase price.

Sellers are not allowed to list the property for sale when lease options are used. Furthermore, lease options contracts couldn't be sold or assigned without being approved by both parties. If a tenant defaults on their contract or cannot acquire bank financing when the contract expires, they forfeit all the funds used toward the purchase.

Lease purchase agreements are the second type and are the most complicated lease-to-own contract. Buyers are legally allowed to buy real estate once the contract expires. If they happen to default on the purchase contract, they might have to deal with legal consequences. So, it's important to know all the risks involved before they enter into a lease-purchase option agreement.

Buyers must perform due diligence by acquiring real estate assessments as well as home inspections. Buyers must get comparable sales reports in order to figure out the fair market value. Sellers are able to choose to lock-in the purchase price when lease-purchase agreements are drafted or ask buyers to pay fair market value once the contract expires.

Buyers are able to offer a lump sum down payment or pay it in instalments. For instance, the seller requires a $30,000 down payment but lets the buyer pay $20% of it upfront and extend the remaining throughout the term of the agreement.

A part of the rent money is put toward the purchase value. Sellers hardly assign 100 per cent of rent money, but this happens in some cases. Averagely, sellers save 10% to 40% of the monthly rent.

Buyers that have poor credit score should participate in credit repair strategies in order to boost their credit scores and get rid of the bad credit in order for them to qualify for a home mortgage loan once the effect of the lease option finishes.

Steps to Acquiring Lease Option Agreement

Selling real estate on lease option agreement is a great technique allowing you to tap into a big sea of people that are interested in buying a property but for some reason, are not quite able to make the purchase at the moment. If you're one of these people, here are the steps to follow to get into this agreement.

Step 1: Find the Property to Buy

Search for properties in your neighbourhood or in a desirable location somewhere else. Homeowners sometimes advertise their houses as lease-to-own. You may want to drive around and search for signs. Usually, the sign will tell the purchase price as well as the monthly rent. Also, search online sites for these sort of properties as well.

Step 2: Research the Home and the Owner

Check the reason why the homeowner is selling it. Make sure that the seller is a motivated seller and want to get rid of the property quickly because of maybe wanting a bigger house, or the property has negative equity, or they're moving to a new place for work, etc. Watch out for the signs the owner is facing financial trouble. Remember that if the owner goes bankrupt while you are leasing it, they will probably lose the house and you will also be evicted at the same time. Because of this, you have to make sure that the seller is financially stable.

Step 3: Analyse Tax Records

You are able to acquire property tax records from the tax assessor's office. See to it that the person you have been working with is really the owner. There are times when the person who faces you is a fraudster and just pretending to be the owner.

Step 4: Get an appraisal

It's important to know how much the house is worth, in case you end up buying it at the end of the lease. Get a referral to an appraiser from the real estate agent. You can also search the directory of the American Society of Appraisers.

Step 5: Have the Home Inspected

See if there are any defects in the home now – whether they are major or minor. It's not nice to start staying there and then realize that the house has a serious structural defect. You can get a real estate agent to do the inspection, which may cost you between $300 and $600.

Step 6: Review the title report

A title report is going to tell you how long the seller has the house to his name. Preferably, the seller owned the property for years already. Someone who has owned the property for a long time must have equity built up in the home and are possibly more stable.

Step 7: See if You Will Qualify for a Mortgage

You do not need a mortgage while you're renting. But you will need it later if you choose to purchase the house at the end of the lease period. Just make sure your credit is not so bad by this time, or you won't get qualified.

Step 8: Negotiate the Purchase Price

Negotiate the price you want to pay if you want to buy the property at the end of the lease. Remember it's an option to buy not an obligation, and the contract you set up for this should state this.

Step 9: Close the Deal

Closing the deal can be a lengthy process. The lender may want an appraisal, inspection, and of course, the title report. You will need to review any disclosures from the seller regarding the defects in the property. If everything goes well, you must close about 45 days after you exercise the option.

2.3.2 Real Estate Wholesaling

Another option you can use when investing in real estate business with limited funds is wholesaling. This is one of the methods you can use to generate money without ever owning property or putting up a huge amount of money for the home. You are able to tie up the property by putting it under contract for a minimal fee, and then you sell it for a higher price compared to the price that was accepted when you put it under the agreement.

Wholesaling is a short-term investing method. Many people think that it's the same as fixing and flipping, but the two have significant differences. Wholesaling real estate is the way to go for those who don't have a lot of money on the table; the downside of this, however, is the confusion it can cause as well as the complicated legality and contracts. When becoming a wholesaler, always stay compliant to the rules and regulations to avoid getting into any lawsuits etc.

Steps to Real Estate Wholesaling

Step 1: Search for a Property to Wholesale

The best type of properties to wholesale are the distressed ones. This is because you can buy them under market value. Distressed properties are the ones in critical condition or the ones that the owners want to get rid of as soon as possible. Choosing this type of property will let you sell the property at a higher price, giving you a big return on investment.

Step 2: Set an Offer that will Convince the Owner to Sell It

The moment you have identified a property with a good deal, the next step is to convince the property owner to sell it to you. This is a very important step since it is going to help you secure the properties to wholesale and generate a profit.

When you're approaching the homeowner, it's important to carry it out it in a delicate way. Because a wholesaler isn't a traditional real estate expert, they'll have to gain the trust of the homeowner before going through. This could be done by being polite, professional, and punctual when meeting the homeowner.

Step 3: Sign the Contract

The homeowner will have to approve and sign the contract. You can create your own contract, but if you want it to look more professional, you can hire a local agent or attorney to set up the contract for you. The latter is the better option so you can make sure that the contract follows the Agreement of Sale.

Step 4: Search for the Right People in the Team

There are three important team members you need to have to run this project better. These are a contractor, title company, and an appraiser. With these people on your team, you can assure that you can maintain the company's level of professionalism and that you can run your business according to how it should be. Having these people in your team will help you save time and money in due course.

Step 5: Evaluate the Needs of the Property for Renovation

By evaluating what renovations are needed in the property, you will know the expenses and make sure they will work according to your plan to make money off the deal. A property that requires renovations can potentially earn you more money. This margin will also help you generate money. That's why it's important that you know how much renovation the property needs as this gives you an idea of how much return you'll get from it.

Step 6: Find a Buyer

You now found a property to wholesale, hired the right professionals to help you, and are aware of what repairs the property needs. Finding the buyer will be the next step. You're not looking for a family or a first-time buyer, but rather, it is going to be an investor or a contractor who wants to buy the property to repair it.

You have to find a buyer immediately because there is going to be a settlement date on the contract that you have to follow. When the potential buyers start calling you about the property, save their info, even if it turns out that your property is not what they are looking for.

Step 7: Negotiate a Deal with the Buyer

When you've finally found the buyer that is interested in buying the property, negotiating the deal would be the next step. It's important to negotiate as it is going to help you determine how much money you will make from this deal. The difference between how much you bought the property for and what you are wholesaling it for will be the total amount of profit you make.

While you're negotiating with the buyer, use the estimate of the contractor to your advantage. Tell the potential buyer that you have other buyers that are interested in the property, so if they want to buy it, they must act fast. The buyer must leave a deposit, which can be held in escrow until things get settled.

Step 8: Closing on the Wholesale Property

Now to the final step… The closing, also known as the settlement, has to be made at the title company's office and is going to last about one and a half-hour. Both parties are going to be there as the deed is being transferred to its new owner. When it's done, it is going to be the completion of the wholesale deal.

Chapter 3

How To Find Lucrative Properties

All good investors are aware of the importance of knowing how to find and choose properties that are going to be profitable. So, whether you're a seasoned investor or simply starting out, finding where to find a property is something many real estate investors may find challenging. Here are different effective ways you can follow:

I. Search for a Beginner Property with Good Potential

You don't have to go too far to find the best property. The first place to look at is your own town, your own area. You are familiar with it, so you'll know which areas are good and which are the ones that are bad. You are far less likely to lose money when you are familiar with your way around. Starting small is the best way to be a real estate shark. In this industry, going big is likely to lead to going home.

Set a Clear Goal

Setting a clear goal shouldn't be too difficult. Figure out as early as possible how much money you are willing to invest and how much of a return you are trying to reach by the end of the year. For example, your goal could be to get at least 50% of what you spent by the end of the year from the time the business starts spending money. Your goal can surely help you determine the type of property suitable for you.

Make Sure that Everything You Are Dealing with is Legal

This might be surprising, but a lot of property owners rent out their units in places they are not allowed to legally. So, you have to make sure that the rental is legal by confirming it at the registrar's office.

Buy the Neighbourhood, Not the House

A house of the same size and quality only a couple of blocks away can be worth 20% more. All towns have a good and bad neighbourhood, and you want to choose a good neighbourhood that your budget can afford.

Don't Settle for the First One You see

It's so easy to fall in love with the first property we see, but try to hold back because you might find better ones! It's best to look at all the options available and then shortlist all the ones you like until you find the one you think is best for you.

Get Help from a Local Broker

You can check all the news ads and all the websites that state the available properties in your area, but no one knows better than a local broker. If you do great research, they surely can do it better!

II. Know What to Check Out

Before putting in money into any property for sale, make sure you know the history of it. Based on that, you can make predictions on how it is going to turn out after you buy it.

Don't Think the Taxes Will Stay the Same

Taxes change annually and could go up drastically after buying it.

Know the Factors in the Cost of Your Tenants Moving in and Out

The huge surprise for most new landlords is the costs of tenant turnover, such as advertising for a new tenant, cleaning fees, agent fees, repainting, and adding new basic furniture.

Get an Insurance Quote Beforehand

You have to keep in mind that insurance on an investment property is much more expensive compared to the house insurance.

Find Out the Realistic Maintenance Expenses

If the property is made of brick, then you probably wouldn't have to paint, and you don't have to spend on maintaining the condition of the wood. Of course, it is a lot easier to maintain a smaller property compared to a bigger one. On top of that, more units mean more money being spent. When you buy a property that is located miles away, then it means you'd have to spend more money on gas to drive around.

III. Get Yourself a Good Partner

Searching for a good business partner is as tough as finding a good property. The best real estate partners you can have are the ones who carry the traits and skills you don't have. If you are good with negotiation but don't know much about finance, then find one that is good with it. Or if you are good with marketing but find managing clients overwhelming, find the one that's an expert in it. A lot of today's best real estate partnerships are a combination of someone with a lot of money and someone who has the knowledge to run it.

Chapter 4

HOW TO SPOT A GOOD DEAL

Whether you're planning to flip a house, buying a property to eventually turn it into rental space, or do something completely different to it, one thing is for sure: it has to be a great deal. Let me give you some simple tips that will guide you in finding the better deals in real estate investment regardless of what your plans are.

1. Consider purchasing a bank-foreclosed property

When someone was not able to pay a mortgage, and it has been a long period of time, the lender will eventually repossess the property and kick out the occupants. When the home is empty, the lender will then list the house for sale on the market, with the help of a local real estate agent to list it.

2. Be the first to make the offer

In the world of real estate, you have to keep in mind that the higher offer is not the only one that always wins, but the one that offers first. So, if you're seeking a great deal, make sure to be the faster one! Get pre-approved by a bank right away, jump off the property you think is best for your intentions. Ask the real estate agents you know to inform you about the latest offerings available in the market in case you find them interesting. And don't waste your time and check it out right away and send off an offer.

3. Connect with absentee owners in private

Due to the high demand of the real estate market, it becomes more challenging to find great deals in real estate. In several areas, a single house listed on the market might receive a dozen or more offers within its first few days.

And with this situation, one of the best kinds of sellers to find is absentee owners, which simply means a person who owns a property but does not live there anymore. These people could be landlords or owners who inherited the property and are just uncertain about what to do with them.

There are many different ways you can find them, and here are those ways:

❖ Drive around and search for houses that may look vacant

❖ Buy a public record list from an aggregate-list site like ListSource.com

❖ Search on craigslist or even post an ad on it saying you're searching for abandoned properties

4. Know what good deals really are

Last, but not least, you have to learn how to determine whether the deal is good or bad! Don't settle for the first thing you find as you'll almost always find more options. Remember that a "good deal" doesn't always mean the cheaper one. You have to look at everything that comes with the deal, like where is it located, how much renovation is needed, or how clean the title is.

Whether you're planning to purchase an investment property, purchase a home to give a roof to your family, or purchase a property for other reasons, always keep in mind that in order to make money, you need to spend money. Remember that finding a good deal is key to having quick equity.

4.1 What to Look for When Looking for Real Estate

Continuous income, stability, appreciation, tax benefits, great returns – the arguments for investing in long-term, hold-to-rent real estate definitely make a lot of sense. And while buying a property is always exciting, it can also be pretty scary, stressful, and more than a bit painful as you make your way through approvals, paperwork, and "hoops" of different shapes and sizes.

In order to help you navigate the process a bit easier, here are important things to look for when looking for real estate.

- **A Great Location**

"Location, location, location…" It is pretty obvious why people put so much importance on the location of the real estate. First of all, a good location is the key to getting a good ROI. It also determines the amount of rent you earn, the quality of your renter, and the vacancy rate you may experience.

A neighbourhood that gives you access to many amenities would be your best bet when you are planning to hold-and-rent. Great schools, a big job market, public transportation, recreation area, shopping centres, restaurants, post offices, libraries, medical centres, and entertainment places are some of the things that are going to make your rental appealing to your prospective tenants.

- **Practical Amenities**

If you are new to the real estate industry, you find it tempting to choose your investment property based on your emotions. That is a common trap, and it is something you don't want to fall into. Keep in mind that you are not going to be living in this rental yourself, so it wouldn't make sense to prioritize your taste and preferences. You might want a unit with a bigger kitchen, but are you sure that it's something that every tenant would want? What if your first tenant would be a busy bachelor who would rather order meals? Do you think the money you paid for having a bigger kitchen is going to be worth it? As long as the amenities are complete, it is enough. This is not to say that you must avoid units with more space – that's still going to be a big bonus, but that shouldn't be a priority.

- **Low Maintenance**

There are investment properties that would take more time to maintain than others. Some of these are student rentals and vacation rentals. Properties in low-quality areas that are not in good shape also have higher turnover rates and will need more work on your part.

Most of the time, the most low-maintenance properties attract stable, long-term tenants. These possibly wouldn't be the flashiest investments on the market, but it's okay. It's always better to opt for something strong and steady, rather than be a flash in the pan.

- **The Potential to Appreciate**

A good investment is a rental property that brings a lot of value. As an investor, you must appraise the property on two levels: the first is to value it when you buy it and the second is to value it when you're selling it.

When you're buying it, look deep into its potential and envision how you can turn it into something that will generate income. How much more can you charge on it after laying new layers of paint on the walls? What about when you replace the curtains with new ones? By appreciating it even before you bought it, it is going to be easier for you to appreciate it when it's ready for selling.

- **Normal, Through and Through**

Long-term, hold-to-rent properties could be a great and stable investment – as long as you are smart. Otherwise, you may find yourself in a high-risk situation quickly. When it comes to long-term rentals, "smart" means "normal." It's not your goal to be the next HGTV star. What you want is to have a steady, low-risk investment.

What "normal" means is that you need to look for something more practical, in good, presentable shape – a place people would want to live in. A good example of something practical is a 3-bedroom, 2-bath house with a good layout for a family, located near major employment centres, shopping market, and school. On the other hand, what is considered impractical is buying a gorgeous updated Victorian property that has a big backyard located in the middle of nowhere.

In finding the right real estate investment, there is one mantra you need to follow: Stick to the basics. While they might not look very enticing at first glance, they could actually be something extremely exciting only if you look at them deeper.

4.2 The Importance of Not Letting Emotions Affect You When Buying Properties

According to real estate agents, emotional mistakes are very common among home investors, who pay too much for their "dream homes" because they put too much of their emotions when buying a property.

However, there's no point for buyers to beat themselves up for getting emotional throughout this process. Buying a property or a house is usually the biggest purchase a person will ever make. So, often, homebuyers need a person or two to stand by their side and remind them how they shouldn't let their emotions decide their investment.

Logic and emotions are two natural traits that clash when combined together when one is shopping. And being able to know how both traits can affect the process of your decisions while shopping for a property can ease stress away and let you feel in control of the buying process.

Now let's take a look at how emotions affect the buying process and how it shouldn't be tolerated. Buyers have to be aware of emotional mistakes a lot of their fellow investors make.

4.2.1 Common emotions that prompt us to make the purchase

Generally, there are three emotional factors that trigger people in making the wrong decisions. Those include the following:

Pain: It becomes the motivating factor why we search for a home in the first place. It might be that a new member of the family is coming, one has to relocate for work, or a person needs a new source of income.

Promise: This motivating factor carries new hope and joy in the future, like having wealth from a continuous source of income from the rental business.

Fear: This emotion makes the person worried that he might be spending a handsome amount of money on something that is not worth it.

A quick emotional attachment

When a potential investor walks into the house, chances are he might fall in love with it right away. They start imagining themselves living it in, changing something in the house to make it the way they want. They start to look way ahead into the future, imagining themselves years after buying it. The tour can easily trigger future hopes and thoughts. On the other hand, if you can't feel these emotions, then it's probably because there's no instant emotional attachment.

Romanticized notions

Most of the time, buyers love to hear the history of the property, particularly about the previous owners, what they do, where they are now, and why did they move. This makes them feel and imagine themselves being in those people's shoes.

Cultural beliefs

Some people base their decisions on certain beliefs or superstitions. For example, in China and Japan, number 9 is believed to be an unlucky number. On top of this, many traditional Chinese families strictly follow Feng Shui.

Influence of colours

Colours can trigger feelings and emotions in people. And that even means paying more money for a house to be painted in specific colours. For example, recent data support the idea that houses that have bathrooms with light pale blue to soft periwinkle blue bathrooms sold for more than the ones with other colours. It's normal for people to want to feel peaceful when they are in their own homes. Furthermore, statistics show that wall interiors painted with neutrals colours such as blue and grey have a better appeal and might indicate that the house was well-taken care of by its old owners.

On the other hand, properties that are painted with darker colours like terracotta sold for way less than the expected price.

There's no denying the fact that emotions can make potential home buyers make bad decisions in investment. This happens more often than you imagine. Some people just pay more than what the properties actually cost.

When homebuyers let their emotions go crazy, it surpasses the logic entirely. But remember that at the end of the day, emotions will always play a part in buying a property; you just have to learn how to limit and control them.

Why We Shouldn't Let Emotions Rule Us

One of the biggest challenges in the sale of a property is the emotional reactions of both parties. It does not matter if you're the buyer, seller, or even the realtor. If either party allows emotions to run the day, things may go differently from how you originally planned them, and it may get ugly.

For the one who is selling the property, emotions root from the fact that they have lived in the home for some time. They built priceless memories in their property – that is where they raised their kids, built their dreams, and that has been their safe, comfortable place for years. In other words, sellers don't see the property as just a piece of land with a house on it. They see it as something that makes them who they are, which they have to let go and move on from. This personal attachment causes tangled feelings when a buyer offers any bad comments about the property.

For buyers, on the other hand, emotions result from the conscious or subconscious nervousness about having to pay a big amount of money. Whether you admit it or not, it is pretty scary to commit to paying to something that costs more than what you already have in the bank. Of course, this emotion may come as a red flag. For example, you feel like the seller is pushing you too much into buying the property, your feelings might tell you that there might be something wrong with the property that's why the seller is trying to sell it fast.

So, whether you are planning to buy or sell a property, make sure that you can let go or at least control your emotions. Remember that this is a business transaction, and in business, logic comes first.

4.2.2 Which Properties Are the Best to Buy for Rentals?

One of the biggest decisions investors make when looking for property for rentals is to choose which property is the best for this purpose. After all, you will have many options. That's why choosing the one that you must buy should be well-thought-out, and there should be no room for rushed decisions.

But in this chapter, we will talk about the two most common options when it comes to rental properties: condo and a single-family home. Which one is the better option to invest? Let's explore their features, pros and cons, and other factors that will help you decide.

Which one is better? Condo vs Single Family Home

Before getting to the conclusion as to whether condos or single-family home would be a better option for real estate investment, let's look at each type of property first.

❖ **Condos**

This is a type of rental property that is a multi-family housing unit and is also known as a condominium. This kind of property can be either built as an apartment building or similar to a single-family house.

Usually, the condos are set up as separate units in a bigger residential real estate building. The major difference between apartments, however, lays in the ownership of this type of investment properties. While apartments are usually owned by one person or company, the units in the condos are sold individually.

Another thing is that condos are built as detached houses. And while this is the case, they're considered a different type of investment property compared to single-family homes. That is because even when condos are built as detached homes, they share common facilities like pools, gym, etc.

❖ **Single Family Homes**

Single-family homes are single detached houses. These types of properties are entirely detached from any other real estate properties. Single-family homes usually have a private yard and direct access to the street. Furthermore, these residential properties don't share any common areas, and community maintenance is not necessary.

The previous characteristics of every property type are just a little part of the subject of condo vs single-family home. In order to have the full picture of the matter, it would be necessary to be familiar with the pros and cons of both rental property types. By knowing these, deciding as to whether you should buy a condo or a single-family home would be much easier.

Advantages and Disadvantages of Buying a Condo

❖ **Affordable Real Estate**

One of the top reasons as to why condos are considered one of the best real estate investment option is the fact that they are affordable. These income properties are fairly affordable on the standard of the real estate market, especially in comparison to single-family properties. Even beginner low-budget real estate investors can get started by investing in condos and developing their rental property business even more.

❖ Rental Property Management and Maintenance

The management and maintenance are one of the top reasons why investing in a condo is a very popular option. Because the property shares common areas together with other units, an investor isn't required to maintain all of these areas. The job is usually done by community service providers. So, the landlord must spend time and money in the condo unit itself and pay extra fees for the maintenance of common areas. This is not the case with single-family homes.

❖ Higher Demand in the Rental Market

Last but not least, condos have higher demand, therefore finding tenants for them is easier. That means that they bring high occupancy rates and steady rental income. This phenomenon is not rocket science – this is just due to the fact that today's young generation prefers renting multifamily units. Millennials start to think about starting a family and renting a bigger home only later in life. The high demand leads to a high ROI for condominiums.

Of course, just as with everything else, choosing a condo for rental also comes with some disadvantages.

❖ Rental Restrictions

First of all, condos usually come with rental restrictions, which might be imposed by the on-site community, for example. A lot of people don't want tenants on the premises of the multifamily homes because tenants might create noise and do damage to the common areas, etc. So, you have to carefully consult with the other owners or the HOA before starting to rent out your new property.

❖ **Real Estate Investment Loans**

Another problem you might encounter is when you are using real estate investment loans. While condos are normally affordable, financing them is not easy. In fact, you might find it difficult to get traditional mortgage lenders to give you the money for you to use in these properties. There are mortgage lenders that require a high down payment, while some even request the owner to live in the property for a certain period of time before they are allowed to buy it.

4.2.3 Advantages and Disadvantages of Investing in Single Family Home Rentals

❖ Higher Real Estate Appreciation

The biggest advantage of investing in a single-family home is real estate appreciation. By running this type of property as your rental business, you're going to be in full control of maintaining and upgrading the rental property. Through this, you can always increase the resale value of this investment. For this reason alone, a lot of property investors believe that single-family homes are the better rental investment.

❖ Type of Tenant

As mentioned earlier, multifamily units are typically rented by younger people. Sometimes, it is the case that such tenants misbehave and damage the property in some sort of way. When it comes to single-family homes, on the other hand, the tenants are usually young families who would like to settle down. This might give a real estate investor confidence that the rental property is going to be taken good care of.

❖ The Freedom Single-Family Rentals Give

Of course, the freedom that comes with this type of investment is a big advantage. You can rent out the property to whoever you want. You can manage and keep the rental property however you want.

But then again, there are also a few disadvantages that come with investing in single-family homes. Here are some of them.

❖ Vacancies

Because condos are more in demand, it might not be as easy for you to find tenants for your property. So, this just means that once the unit goes vacant, there's a high chance for the property to stay like this for a while. Investing in a few multifamily units leads to lower vacancy rates. Since purchasing multiple single-family homes is a bit more complicated, it's not always easy to avoid negative cash flow from time to time.

❖ Cost

Last of all is the cost of such an investment. Single-family homes are difficult to finance at first because of their initial property value. Furthermore, the maintenance and renovation of the property are also more expensive compared to condos.

Conclusion

Both condos and single-family homes would be great investment opportunities for investors looking for rental properties. Just make sure that you are aware of the pros and cons, and from there, you can decide which one works best for you.

4.2.4 What below market value means?

Below the market can refer to any kind of investment or purchase that is made at a below the market price. In the world of investment trading, a below the market order is an order to purchase or sell a security at a price that is lower compared to the current market price. In wider terms, below the market may also refer to the price or rate that's lower compared to the current prevailing conditions in an open market. Services or goods that are offered at a lower price compared to the "going," or typical, rate could be considered as below the market.

Purchases made under below the market conditions are good to the buyer since they can obtain goods, investments, or services at a price that's lower than the going rate. Below the market is a common term that could be used by investors as well as investment traders.

Below the Market Trade Orders

Traders and investors might have several platforms available when looking to execute a trade. Institutional investors could usually access different public and non-public trading centres. Retail investors are usually going to execute their trades through a discount brokerage platform or ask their broker to place a trade. In most situations, all investors have the choice to choose the maximum price they want to pay for something.

In a below the market order, an investor who would like to try to meet a better price or position can enter an order to purchase securities at a price that's below the market. In general, trading platforms will lay down the order with a selected price as a limit order.

In a limit order, the investor offers a maximum price they're willing to pay to buy a security. Putting a below the market limit order is going to give a much higher risk of being unsettled in the open market. If the day's price on the specified security never goes below its current trading price or in case it goes up, the limit order wouldn't be placed, and the investor wouldn't take ownership in the security. If the limit order to purchase is filled, the order is going to be placed at the specific price. There are trades in which only a part of the shares might be bought if the broker can't identify sellers for a full lot of requested shares.

Limit orders that let investors identify below the market price for purchasing security will vary from standard market orders. Standard market orders are usually a defaulted order type of trading platform.

Capital gains

Capital gain is a rise in the value of a capital asset real estate or investment, which gives it a higher worth compared to the purchase price. You wouldn't realize the gains until the asset is sold. A capital gain might be considered short-term or long-term and have to be claimed on income taxes.

Understanding Capital Gains

While capital gains are usually associated with funds and stocks because of their inherent price volatility, a capital gain may take place on any security that's sold for a price higher than the purchase price that was paid for it. Realized capital losses and gains happen when an asset is sold, which leads to a taxable event. Sometimes, unrealized gains and losses are referred to as paper gains and losses, which reflect growth or decline in value of the investment that hasn't yet triggered a taxable event.

A capital loss is sustained when there's a decrease in the capital asset value compared to the purchase price of the asset.

4.2.5 Tax Consequences of Capital Gains and Losses

Tax-conscious mutual fund investors have to determine a mutual fund's unrealized gathered capital gains, which are considered as a percentage of its net assets before you invest in a fund with a significant unrealized capital gain factor. This circumstance is referred to as a capital gains exposure to the fund. When distributed by a fund, capital gains are a taxable obligation for the investors of the fund.

Short-term capital gains happen on securities held for a year or less. These gains are taxed as ordinary income derived from the person's tax filing status and attuned gross income. Long-term capital gains are normally taxed at a lower rate compared to regular income. 20% is the long-term capital gains rate in the highest tax bracket. However, 15% is the most common qualifying number for tax-payers.

Capital Gains Distribution by Mutual Funds

Mutual funds that have amassed realized capital gains through the year should distribute those gains to the shareholders. A lot of mutual funds distribute capital gains at the end of the year.

People who are receiving the distribution acquire a 1099-DIV form, which explains the amount of the capital gain distribution and how much is considered short-term and long-term. Once the mutual fund makes a capital gain or bonus distribution, the net asset value (NAV) goes down by the amount of the distribution. A capital gains distribution doesn't affect the total return of the fund.

4.2.6 Understanding ROI in real estate (return on investment)

One important factor that many savvy real estate investors look at when choosing which properties might be profitable for them is the rate of return on rental property.

Return on investment or ROI is an accounting term that defines the percentage of invested money that is earned after the deduction of associated expenses. This is something that could be confusing for a layperson to understand. However, the formula is as simple as this:

$$ROI = \frac{Gain - Cost}{Cost}$$

where:

Gain = Investment gain

Cost = Investment cost

But while the equation seems easy enough to calculate, with real estate, several variables, which include repair and maintenance expenses and means of figuring leverage, come into play, which could affect ROI numbers. In a lot of cases, the ROI is going to be higher if the cost of the investment is lower.

When buying a property, the terms of financing could significantly affect the price of the investment. But then again, using resources such as a mortgage calculator could help you save money on the investment expenses by helping you find favourable interest rates.

Calculating ROI on real estate could be simple or complicated, depending on all the variables involved. In a healthy economy, investing in real estate, may it be residential and commercial, has proven to be extremely profitable. Even during a recessionary economy, when prices go down and cash is scarce, a lot of bargains in real estate are available for investors with the money to invest. When the economy gets back on its feet, as it invariably does, a lot of investors will reap a striking profit.

Chapter 5

SALES & NEGOTIATION TECHNIQUES

If you really want to get into the game and earn real money in the world of real estate investment, then you should master the art of negotiation. What many people don't actually understand about real estate is that it's a business, and therefore whether you are a real estate investor, businessman, lawyer, or even a housewife, negotiations are an important part of life and are most certainly key to attaining success. Ask any successful individuals, and you will see that, for the most part, they've become skilled at negotiation and can normally work things in their odds.

Not everyone knows how negotiation works, but this skill could be learned by anyone as long as they are eager to learn. Along with the drive to succeed and an enthusiasm for learning, anyone who wants to expand his horizons is able to open his doors to very prolific real estate negotiations and deals that can change his life for the better. After all, not everyone is easy to deal with; that's why the art of negotiating is always going to come in handy as a person walks through the journey of life.

Mastering the art of negotiation is usually more complicated than it seems. Good negotiation is one in which both parties could actually gain something valuable. When a party loses while the other one wins, then the wrong negotiating strategies must have been used. Good deals must always benefit both parties, as there might come the point in time when the person you are dealing with can significantly help you in the future.

Let's take this case, for example. A real estate investor wants to sell a property to a buyer who's searching for a house to live in. This investor might want to sell the house at a very high price while the buyer is looking for quality and value for money. This is a give and take scenario and will make both parties win in the situation. The real estate investor can get a high price for the property if the house he is selling is in great shape and the condition preferred by the buyer. The investor earns from the deal while the buyer gets the house that he wants.

While negotiations are a lot more evident in real estate and business deals, this is something we do unconsciously every day. We do it when asking for more time at work. We do it when inviting someone at a party. It is an important skill that people must learn. When done properly, negotiating could be turned into profits and a very comfortable life.

There are people who learn how to negotiate well when they are exposed to individuals from all walks of life. A job that lets someone meet a lot of people significantly helps in improving one's negotiating skills. This, together with reading good books and going to related seminars or classes, helps in developing negotiation skills.

Even if you're trying to avoid them, negotiations are the key to getting what you want and offering a great future for your family. When you learn the art of negotiating, it's going to be a skill that you will always have with you for the rest of your life. It most definitely provides you with a better advantage in any situation you are in.

5.1 How to Negotiate During a Real Estate Transaction

The goal is to have an agreement on the terms of the deal, which include price, timelines, eventualities, and items that might carry with the property. Remember that there will be continuous negotiation until the deal is closed. Here are some scenarios buyers and sellers should prepare for.

Price

Both sellers and buyers would try to negotiate the best price possible for their benefits, and there are many possible reasons for this. Of course, the seller wants to sell the property as expensive as possible while the buyer, on the other hand, would want to pay the lowest amount possible. They usually meet somewhere in between. Buyers don't want to pay more than what the property usually costs, while the seller, on the other hand, wants to make sure that he's getting the right amount of money from the property he is selling.

Closing costs

The prepaid closing expenses for their mortgage have to be paid by the buyer. This is the money that the mortgage lender has in escrow for things such as taxes and insurance. It's acceptable for the buyer to ask a seller to pay for the entire closing costs or up to how much the lender is allowed to pay a contribution. This could be up to 3% of what's included in the mortgage. If a buyer asks the seller to make a franchise on his behalf, they are likely going to need to pay a higher asking price.

Closing date

Sellers are allowed to negotiate for speed when they have to get their capital out of the home quickly, and closing dates are going to affect buyers' monthly cash flow when they own the home. Remember that when a buyer closes on the property, he skips the payment for a mortgage for the following month. They probably want to close at the starting part of the month so that they skip the following month.

Financing contingencies

Many transactions end up being cash; that's why sellers do not tie up their property for 1 to 2 months, which is what is needed when there is a financing contingency in place. Buyers that are trying to compete with all-cash offers have to know if they are capable of dropping the financing eventuality that will make the closing timeline shorter. This is possible for the buyer if they get their mortgage entirely approved before making an offer.

Home warranty

When it comes to the home warranty, the seller can ask or even demand this or the seller can voluntarily offer this. This is a protection plan that covers the appliances and systems of the home, like hot water heater and A/C in the event these things break or require repair or maintenance.

Leaseback

There's no denying the fact that moving to a new place is a process that is highly stressful. If a seller requires a bit of extra time to get into their new home, buyers can offer a zero-cost rent-back for 1 to 3 months to convince the seller to accept the offer over others. Giving the buyer peace of mind is a very effective negotiating tactic.

Home repairs

When the house requires a lot of repairs, this is going to be an opportunity for the buyer to negotiate a lower price. When a home is outdated with appliances that no longer work, cracked walls, or popped ceilings, a buyer could ask for a lower price due to the cost of repairs needed to be done. If the seller doesn't want to make any repairs on the property, then it should be advertised "as is".

Appraisal contingency

If the buyer is getting a mortgage, waiving the appraisal contingency is possible for the buyer to do. But this is only when they make good on the amount of cash to close if for some reason the appraisal falls short, and the bank will lend them just enough money based on an appraised value.

Furniture

Personal properties such as chandeliers, patio furniture, cabinets, and window treatments are also up for grabs. If the seller has a lot of furniture in the property and the buyer happens to want to keep them, then negotiation may ensue. Whatever's not included in the deal has to be stated once the contract is finalized. Otherwise, more negotiations may ensue.

Appliances

There are some appliances that may come with the property. These include built-in appliances like dishwasher, stove, and microwave. These appliances are a good tool for bumping up the value of the property and play a good role in negotiation.

5.2 Understanding A Motivated Seller and How to Add Value to A Deal

Real estate investments for commercial purposes can be categorized depending on the kind of deals used on them. These categories are the following:

CORE

Because they normally target stabilized, secured investments on the market, the core investments are known to be the least risky option. These include properties that have long-term leases on them rented by tenants with high credit score and properties that are located in extremely in-demand locations. These buildings are usually well kept and need little to no improvements for the new owner. So, as expected, these real estate properties don't experience great appreciation in value but instead offer steady income and very low to no risk at all.

This form of investment is perfect for investors who need capital preservation and long hold periods and usually allows for low leverage attainments. While Core investments are seemingly not as popular as the commercial real estate options, many people still choose them due to the low risk they offer.

Even though this form of investment is typically not as liquid as securities offered on an exchange in commercial real estate, they're usually considered the most liquid assets when it comes to opportunistic value addition projects since they're attractive, steady, and highly in-demand assets.

VALUE-ADD

Value-add commercial real estate investments is a form of investment that usually focuses on properties that aspire to increase their cash flow despite having in-place cash flow. This is done by making improvements on the property. This could mean doing some sort of physical improvements on the property that can justify the higher rent. But this must also intend to improve the standard of living of the people renting the property. When the property's net income was successfully improved by the operator, the next step is to sell the asset to get the ensuing appreciation in value.

OPPORTUNISTIC

The last in the list is the opportunistic investing. This form of investment involves investing in misjudged and extremely undervalued properties. These are the properties that require a lot of work to reach their full potential market value.

With this type of investment, your goal as an investor is to take a tactical risk to attain out-sized revenues. For this reason, there are many forms of asset investments that come under this category, which includes ground-up developments and emerging and adaptive markets. Opportunistic investments can also be the acquisition of foreclosed properties from banks.

If you choose to invest into this route, you'll need to think in advance and depend on the future of the asset because the returns will come from imminent rental income or the sale the property when the market gets better.

5.3 How to Approach People and Establish Credibility

There are a lot of traits that can help you become successful in this trade. But one of the most important things you need to improve about yourself is your ability to be credible in the eyes of others.

In some ways, your credibility is a higher bar compared to your success. This means that other people look at you as a dependable decision-maker and resource. This will allow others to rely on you because they know they can count on you when they need to trust their business to someone.

Being credible means developing a set of specific qualities – regardless of your role, industry, and organization. Here are some things you need to do if you're serious about being a credible businessman:

❖ **Be reliable.** In order to cultivate credibility, it's important to build trust, earn it, and use it. If people trust you, they wouldn't have a second thought about doing business with you. Remember that in the world of business, there's nothing more important than being trusted by people.

❖ **Be capable.** Be the master of your craft and show people that you are capable of actually doing things that you promised. Be confident and trust your skills, and when people see that, they will follow.

❖ **Be consistent.** Always be consistent in everything you do, say, and think. Show the people that everything you do matches everything you say. Without consistency inside and out, credibility wouldn't happen.

❖ **Be real.** To cultivate credibility, being genuine is necessary; when you are trying to gain trust, you cannot depend on the "fake it till you make it" approach. To be able to successfully establish your credibility, you should be ready for everything that may come your way.

❖ **Be sincere.** Sincerity also plays a huge part. This does not mean saying everything you have in your head but being truthful with everything you say. Practice doing more instead of talking more. Sincerity involves dedication and commitment and the willingness to be unwavering, straightforward, and unmovable.

❖ **Be respectful.** Showing people how you respect their feelings and opinions will mean a lot to them. So, make sure to treat everyone with respect – not because you're expecting something in return, but because that's how it should be.

* **Be responsible.** Being responsible with all your words and actions is one of the keys to being credible. It's also important that you accept that you commit mistakes and you show that you don't have a problem doing anything to fix any mistakes you make. If you're not sure of something, then let people know.

* **Be loyal.** Being able to learn how to show loyalty to people around you is one of the best ways to earn credibility. Keep in mind that loyalty is a mutual commitment, and you must always be willing to show it.

* **Be truthful.** Developing your reputation is a huge part of establishing credibility. Learn how to speak with openness and honesty. You must learn how to be transparent and genuine.

* **Be righteous.** Accept yourself and stop comparing yourself to others – be the righteous person who stands tall to honour the values you believe in. Always try to improve yourself to be a better version of you.

Chapter 6

RAISING FINANCE

Any businessman who is just starting out would attest that gathering funds for a new business venture could be one of the most challenging parts of starting a business. No matter how passionate and eager you are about the business you are trying to start up, without enough funds, it will almost always be nothing.

While searching for an investor is definitely possible, this is not always the best option. Each of us has different situations, so what might work for others might not be a feasible option for you. Here are ways you can use to raise finance.

6.1 If You Have Bad Credit Score

It's true that finding money to start a business is not easy if you have a bad credit score. However, you have to know that this is not impossible. Here are some alternative ways you can follow in order to gather the money you need to start your real estate business.

1. Look beyond bank loans and credit cards. Studies reveal that credit card and bank financing account for only 25% of the total funding requirements of start-up businessmen. This statistic should give you some ease since it suggests that most of the money you need can originate from other resources.

It's possible to find lending agencies that target people with low credit score, but of course, there's always a catch – you can expect that they will charge you higher interest rate. A bank option for people with poor credit scores is a home equity line of credit, although I would be careful about putting my home on the line to fund a risky early-stage endeavour.

2. Borrow from people you know. Did you know that about 50% of the business is funded by people who borrowed money from people they know? These people they know are usually their friends and relative. If you're lucky, your family and friends might trust you enough to lend you some money. They might not even care if you have a poor credit score. If they think you are reliable and that you are capable of being successful in the business you are trying to get into, they might overlook your financial situation.

3. Seek microlenders and online lenders. It's not hard to find nonbank lenders online that are offering microloans to businessmen. These loans usually offer between $5,000 and $25,000. Not only these companies are willing to lend you money, but your payments to them will also be reported to credit bureaus, which means paying them can actually help you rebuild your credit scores. However, make sure to not go to the first one you find. You can always compare the interest rates to find and also read the fine prints.

Because of the benefits they offer, you can expect that they apply higher interest rates than your typical lending companies. For comparison, the average rate on business loans from friends and relative is currently at 7.6%, while the rate was over 12% - 20% at these establishments.

6.2 When You're Unemployed

Unemployment shouldn't stop you from dreaming big. Unlike when you just have a poor credit score, it is hard to find funds for your business when you are unemployed.

Unemployment does not necessarily mean you don't have a chance when it comes to acquiring a loan. While it sounds too good to be true, it's actually possible for someone who doesn't have a job to finance the business they are dreaming of.

What Lenders Seek from Personal Loan Applicants

Of course, when you are applying for a loan, you'll have to go through some sort of screening in order for the lender to know whether you are qualified for the loan or not. Here are some of the things the lender will look at when you are applying for a loan:

❖ **Income:** The most important thing for a lender is to know whether or not you are capable of paying them back. And to know that, they must look through your source of income.

❖ **Credit**: The lender is going to pull your credit file to see your credit score, payment history, as well as utilization.

❖ **Debt-to-income ratio**: They will also check whether or not you have other existing loans. If you happen to have other loans, they will see if your current income can handle the additional loan.

Income is an important part of getting a loan, and that could be a problem when you don't have a job. What you might not have realized is that income from a job is not your only option.

6.3 Alternative Forms of Income

In order to qualify for a personal loan, you will have to show that you have some form of consistent income. Without that, the lender is not likely to grant the loan.

Even though you don't have a job, you can still have other forms of income. Here are some of the options you can use.

- ❖ **Unemployment benefits:** If you're qualified for an unemployment benefit, that still counts as a source of income.

- ❖ **Freelance income:** All forms of income you earn from doing freelancing can count as a source of income.

- ❖ **Investment income:** Another source of income that many people overlook is the money you get from any existing investment.

You have to remember that regardless of which option you have, the lender will most likely perform some sort of income verification.

If you have already applied for a new job and waiting for you to start, that's also a good sign for the lenders that indicate that you can actually afford to pay for the loan. So, if you have a pending contract or certificate of being hired, you can inform the lender about it.

How to Apply for A Loan if You are Unemployed

1. Know your source of income

When applying for a loan, the first thing you have to do is to gather all the documents that explain your current source of income. As mentioned earlier, this could come in the form of other business, existing investments, freelance jobs, or a pending job. You have to prove that you have consisting earnings.

2. Protect your credit

The worst step is to do things that may cause your credit score to drop before you even get approved for a personal loan. This will surely affect your chances of approval as well as your interest rate. In order to protect your credit, see to it that you continue paying all your bills before you hit the due date. Don't rack up big balances on any of your credit cards, as it will increase your debt-to-income ratio and getting approved for a loan will be more difficult for you.

3. Find the right lender for you

There are two important things to look out for when searching for a lender that suits your needs:

- ❖ **Credit score requirements**: Again, there are different types of lenders, and not all of them require applicants to have a soaring credit score. If you have a good credit score, then good! If not, find the ones that don't grant people with a poor credit score.

- ❖ **Amounts offered**: Know how much you need and find a lender that will offer the amount of money you need to start up your business. They will tell you their minimum and maximum, so see if they match up your requirements.

Other Financing Options When You're Unemployed

Get a consignee: By having a consignee on your loan application, the lender is going to check the credit score and income of that person. It will work as if the consignee is also applying for the loan.

Because a consignee is also responsible for the loan the same as the person who borrowed it, most people are hesitant to be one. But then again, it's not impossible to make people agree to be your consignee. You can ask your parents, relatives, or friends to do it for you. They won't hesitate if they know that you are capable of paying the money back.

Credit cards: Credit cards generally are not what you would use to carry a balance due to their interest rates. 0% APR credit cards are a great exception, as they let you pay 0 interest for as long as the intro period of the card lasts. Throughout that time, you just have to make minimum payments. It's also not impossible to find credit companies that wouldn't charge you high-interest fees.

If ever you already applied for a low-interest credit card, this option would be a smart way to pay them off when you don't have a job yet.

Use the equity in your home: Another option could be to refinance your current home and pull out as much equity out of the property as possible. People see this as a bad thing, but not when you're using the money to invest in further assets for cashflow that can pay for your cost of living. Most people are in a rush to pay off their home and be debt-free. But this just leaves them penny less afterwards and still needing to pay bills etc.

Chapter 7

ADDING VALUE TO A PROPERTY

There are people who would buy homes and fall in love with them just the way they are. They would choose not to change anything and keep them the same way. It's different for others though. For them, buying a property is an opportunity. They choose to buy the property, not due to the way it looks or the current features of the house. They choose to buy it because they can see its full potential. They probably had imagined what it would look like when the kitchen was changed or when they put a different kind of sofa in the living room. They already planned the add-ons and changes they want to make in order to make the home more valuable, inviting, and profitable.

This is a good way of thinking for homebuyers, especially those who have the intention of using it as a business investment. First of all, the house would have an improvement that could expand the overall beauty of the place. What used to be just a small piece of land could turn into a pleasing home with many features and amazing landscaping. Regardless of its size, it would have the appeal that future buyers will actually fall in love with. Another advantage is that it would increase the overall value of the property. And the higher the value the property has, the more equity it has and the more money the owner can get when it is used for business purposes. And last of all, the house would have better functionality, and you are able to use it for a long time, especially if you're not planning on reselling it.

Therefore, home improvements would always be a smart idea. But you have to know that it's important to choose the right kind of project that is ideal for your home. Here are different ways to add value to your property:

1. Make it look more appealing

Starting from the outside all the way to the inside, your home should look appealing. The exterior of the property has to make a potential client want to see what's inside. You have to keep the landscaping presentable by keeping it well-maintained. If the yard looks dull compared to the houses next to it, you may want to consider repainting the fences and the door and adding flowers.

When the exterior looks better, you can then move on to the bathroom and kitchen. It's hard to reach your property's highest value if you don't pay enough attention to these two rooms.

And there's no need to invest in heated towel racks or marble floors as well. A small kitchen remodelling adds about 80% of its cost in added value averagely.

The same thing goes for the bathrooms; a midrange remodel – adding new flooring and some updated fixtures add about 70% ROI, while an upscale bathroom remodel attracts about 56% on average.

2. Make it low-maintenance

Because a lot of home buyers are anxious about purchasing a home that will require endless maintenance, replacing a huge component before putting it up for sale or rent might calm fears of an emergency repair in the near future and assist you in getting higher ROI.

Making things easier to clean and maintain can also help you boost the value of the property. You may want to get a new carpet and replace old materials with new ones that don't require much maintenance.

3. Make it more efficient and eco-friendly

The property can have more value to the eyes of the buyers if they can help them save money from energy consumption. You can apply for energy-efficient mortgages or EEMs, which allows you to borrow additional debt to help you upgrade the property and make it more energy-efficient. This kind of loan usually offers low-interest rates.

Properties, especially the ones that are located in places where it can get too hot or too cold, get more value if they have energy conservation features. Ask an expert how you can make the property more efficient, but some of the popular options you can turn to are replacing the windows with double-panel ones and using LED bulbs to illuminate the house at night.

If you want to go big, then you can consider adding a solar panel to your roof. Based on the survey performed by the National Association of Realtors on 39% of their realtors, solar panels increased professed property value. But because solar panels are a huge financial and structural commitment, this only makes sense if you want a long-term benefit from the property like if you are planning to get it rented and not a quick boost in resale value.

To make things clearer for you, you may want to schedule an assessment with a certified energy inspector or your utility company in order to know where your home is wasting energy and what type of upgrades are going to save you the most money.

4. Make it spacious

Square footage has a great effect on the value of a home. One of the main features of a property that indicates its value is its size.

Unsurprisingly, the bigger the property is, the more value is added to it. And even though you don't tell the potential buyer its actual size, this is something that can easily be caught by the eyes. Of course, you can't widen the size of the property unless you bought its surrounding lands, but one thing you can do is to make it spacious. You can add a patio if possible. Or clean up the basement and make it look liveable.

5. Make it smarter

Based on the 2018 survey by Coldwell Banker, safety-enhancing gadgets are on top of the list of "smart" technologies potential clients want in their new homes. These safe and smart devices include fire detectors, thermostats, carbon monoxide detectors, door locks, security cameras, and auto lighting.

While smart tech does not always increase the value of the home, it makes it more appealing. Tech-savvy individuals will be more than willing to pay more if they see how cutting-edge the features are. The good thing about this is that there is not a lot of handyman work involved in this – you only have to install the gadgets, and you are good to go.

7.1 House Flipping: 4 Key Factors that Affect the Costs

The cost to flip a house is equivalent to the sum of the costs of acquisition, repair, sales, and marketing. There are many factors that affect the costs of house flipping. But most of the time, the cost you need to incur to successfully flip a house is about 10% of the price you paid to buy the title of the property.

Again, the total costs to flip a house will greatly depend on the type of project. That is one of the reasons why flipping real estate is super appealing- it is feasible on almost any kind of budget. While it's impossible to tell exactly the amount to spend when flipping a house, there are 4 main expenses that involve this project. These four main expenses of flipping a house are:

Purchase Price of Fix and Flip Property

The property acquisition price is the total money you spent to get the house to your name. In these expenses, you also have to settle the property's purchase amount as well as the closing expenses associated with it. These are the expenses you pay at the settlement of a transaction.

The purchase price is the amount of money you pay to acquire a property. The total purchase price is the payment you make for property itself as well as the land where it is located, and the price depends on the type of property you are buying – if you are buying a condominium type property, then you don't have to pay for the land. The purchase price does not include insurance or taxes, but depending on how the deal is built, it might include custom window treatments, appliances, and light furniture.

There are two things you have to consider when buying a property.

1) The use of comparable properties to see if they match the type of property you are originally looking for; and
2) the costs of after-repair value or ARV.

If you're new to house flipping, calculating the costs can be a little confusing. So, if you want to make it easier, you can start by purchasing properties that only require cosmetic repairs. Dealing with this kind of properties is easier.

Fix & Flip Property Closing Costs

You're the one who's responsible for the closing costs when you buy a property you intend to flip. These expenses will include the transfer taxes, property insurance, share of property taxes, title insurance, as well as the title company fees. The financing would have its own expenses at closing as well if you're the one who's financing the purchase. Both the lender and the real estate agent may offer you a breakdown of the closing expenses.

A conservative rule of thumb is that the closing costs of the buyer will be 5% of the purchase price of the property. If you bought a property amounting $300,000, expect to pay around 5% of $300,000, which is $15,000. So, the $300,000 property will now cost you $315,000. It's important to not forget to include them when trying to calculate the total costs of buying a house to flip because these costs will significantly affect the ROI

Also, it's always a good idea to take photos of the property in its original state and afterwards to give to the valuer of the property to show what you've done. This can help as a valuer may sometimes go away and actually forget your property if they've viewed many others on that day or week.

Cost to Rehab a Property

The cost to rehab a property differs depending on how critical the changes are that need to be done, the size of the property, as well as how much the labour would be. The costs of the rehab include both labour and materials needed.

Fix and Flip Material + Labour Expenses

Don't forget to include delivery costs and construction fees if you had to hire a person to do the job when calculating the total costs of the materials for the project.

The expenses you need to settle on the materials will vary greatly depending on the scope of the rehab project, but they largely fall into two categories:

- ❖ Appliances: Common appliances like a stove, HVAC, refrigerator, etc.

- ❖ Building Materials: The common materials for building a house like paint, nails, etc.

Make sure to also add the labour to make the project possible. They are going to charge you to install all of the materials you bought. There are contractors that charge per hour, but there are also ones that charge per project. This is something you can negotiate for the price and put into a signed contract before the work starts. You might have to hire different labourers depending on your specific needs.

Common labourers include:

- ❖ Day labourers or handymen

- ❖ Electrician

- ❖ General contractor (GC)

- ❖ Landscapers

- ❖ Painters

- ❖ Plumber

The extent of the rehab for the property is the main determining factor on how much it would cost you to flip a house. Again, it's best for beginners to choose properties that only require cosmetic repairs. When you do it successfully, the next projects are going to be easier, and you can eventually choose properties that might have more complicated requirements.

Cosmetic Home Repairs for a Fix & Flip Costs

Cosmetic repairs for the property are minor repairs and improvements that are required to increase the value of the property. You can definitely boost the property's value if you did things right. The faster the project finishes, the lower the costs would be. Labour and material expenses are also lower. But because the property is already in better condition than it was before, you can expect the acquisition costs to be higher.

Chapter 8

COMMON MISTAKES WHEN STARTING REAL ESTATE BUSINESS

There are many things to consider when investing in real estate, but the first important thing to know are the mistakes to avoid on this endeavour. You will want to try to avoid these common mistakes, and you will also want to make sure that you know the important things to do when you're involved in commercial real estate investing. Yes, committing mistakes is almost inevitable, but the more you prepare yourself for it, the more likely it is for you to avoid them.

Mistake #1 - Ignoring the Condition of Your Local Market

One of the major mistakes one can make in commercial real estate investing is to ignore the conditions of the local market. Even though you're investing in a great property, if you choose to do it in a bad market, you are still likely to lose money. On the other hand, a bad property can potentially generate a lot of money if it's within the right area, so demand is always a key factor to remember.

Mistake #2 - Not Doing Proper Due Diligence

Another common mistake that many new investors make when it comes to commercial real estate investing is not taking the time to perform proper due diligence. It can be a good idea to find people that have done similar projects in the area as to the one you're working in. Places like Facebook groups can be a great place to start to find these sort of people.

Mistake #3 - Borrowing Too Much

This is one of the main reasons why an investment business fails. Borrowing more money than you should is a mistake that will certainly lead you to the pit of disaster. You must avoid borrowing too much money unless you are 100% sure that the ROI can afford it within the right timeframe or if you know you have the money to pay for it. Keep in mind that when you invest, you at least have to breakeven, or you will lose money. Of course, your goal is to make sure that you actually generate money on the investment.

Mistake #4 - Not Having Good Plan B, C, and D

A lot of people have found out it out the hard way that you must have a plan B or just an exit plan in case things go south. Make sure that you have strategies for exiting in different unlikable situations. Without multiple exit plans, you might end up being stuck somewhere you don't want to be. It's always a good rule of thumb to imagine the worst-case scenario before getting into a deal and work from there.

Mistake #5 - Doing Business with Bad Partners

While most of the problems you might have to deal with have something to do with the property itself, people could also be your main problem. By partnering with someone who you don't get along with, you are already dealing with a disaster. It's best to get out of that partnership if you see that it's not working out from the beginning. Otherwise, it's just going to be a complete disaster.

Mistake #6 - Taking Too Many Risks

Taking risk is a part of getting into a business. However, there is a fine line between good risk and unhealthy risk. You want to avoid what is called "overreaching" where you go all out on taking risks. Yeah, big deals might probably come at you, but make sure it's something you can realistically deal with.

Learn to crawl before you can run.

Mistake #7 - Owning More Land Than Money

A lot of investors have found themselves committing the mistake of owning more land than they have money to actually cover. If you have a lot of properties at the same time and you are trying to use the gains you get for one to cover what you're losing on another, then you're not doing this business right – you just set yourself on a never-ending cycle. Escape the problem properties right away, even though it might seem difficult. Then, take all of your time and focus on the properties that are going to let you make the maximum amount of earning.

These are all common mistakes. Do yourself a favour and try to avoid them at all costs. However, it's important that you remember that even though you accidentally make a mistake and get yourself in a situation that you didn't want to be in, you can still always fix it and go the right way.

8.1 Things to Do to Prevent Mistakes

While mistakes are inevitable, there are things you can do to prevent them. Here are smart things you can do to avoid common real estate investment mistakes.

❖ **Always Investigate the Deal**

Before closing a commercial real estate deal, it's important to take your time to do some sort of investigation on the deal. This will mean that you need to take the time to do due diligence about any type of property that you're thinking of buying. It's not very smart to get into investing without doing your due diligence – you are likely to end up with a bad deal. Always remember to invest with formulas, not feelings. ROI and areas with demand are key.

❖ Learn from the Mistakes of Others

Learn from people; if you don't know anything, just ask. Like we have said previously, this business model has a great blueprint to learn from. It might involve a lot of test runs, but always try to find out from people that have done what you're about to do. "A smart man learns from his mistakes. A wise man learns from others' mistakes".

❖ Figure Out How Long You Can Wait for a Pay-out

You will have to make sure that you know how long you are able to wait before you actually get a pay-out on the investment you're making. Make sure you have a realistic estimation of how long you can really wait, or you might just end up facing cashflow problems. In time, multiple investments will cover this problem.

Chapter 9

HOW TO MANAGE PROPERTIES

A lot of people think that finding a good deal is the hardest part of investing in real estate. They spend long hours seeking and dealing for the right property. They crunch the numbers over and over again. They make calls over and over again, and walk through a lot of basements and attics. They set their hopes up and then rushed within the same 24 hours. They check the neighbourhood and do their research, check, and then double-check market values. They write up offers, a lot of them with low, almost silly prices. After a lot of hours spent, sacrifices made, offers countered, and displaying much persistence, they have an offer accepted. Now the real work begins.

Step 1: Buy & Repair

Buying the property and getting into good repair is the first step of managing an investment or rental property. Before you open up the property for rentals, there are two important things you have to work on first. The focus of your priority should go to choosing the right property to buy and how you can make it profitable by repairing it.

Step 2: Setting Prices and Expectations

Having control over the rental property and feeling ready to start out the business is not enough to get started. Before you find the tenant who will stay in your property, there's one more important thing you need to get to. And that is to figure out how much you are going to charge for the property and what your expectations are from people who are staying there.

Market Research in Area

You must do your research first before deciding on the rent. Find out the demand for rental properties in the area and know how much is the average rent there. Although you probably have idea what the answers to these questions are after searching for the property there, doing another round of research would be better.

Know the answers to these questions:

- ❖ How much is the average income in the area?

- ❖ What's the average size of the family?

- ❖ What's the average price of the rental?

- ❖ Does the location have any extra-special benefits that you are able to charge more for?

As you know more information about the other rentals on the market as well as the going rates, you can suitably price your rental property.

Tenant Requirements

On top of figuring out the amount to charge to your tenant, another important thing you must figure out is the requirements you have to set for your tenants. You'd have a better opportunity to find high-quality tenants if you determined the requirements you need to look out for.

Here are some things a landlord can ask from the potential tenant:

- ❖ Credit score minimum

- ❖ Employment requirement

- ❖ Minimum income

- ❖ Character reference

- ❖ Previous rental history

- ❖ Smoker or not?

Step 3: Rent Your Property

Now, let's get on the most challenging, yet the most exciting part of the rental process. Now you're ready to hunt for the right tenants you'll take into your property.

Advertising

Advertising your property is another important part of the whole business process – in fact, this is essential regardless of what type of business you have. Advertise anywhere you can; you can invest some money for additional exposure – it's always going to be worth it. You can use popular home sites such as Trulia and Zillow to help you advertise your property.

Finding Quality Tenants

It's important to not accept any tenant who inquires about the property. Make sure that you are renting your property to a high-quality tenant.

So, how can you determine whether the tenant is good or not? A good tenant is someone who pays on time, respects your property, and doesn't cause troubles. Of course, you wouldn't know whether or not an applicant is a good or a bad tenant by simply interviewing them, but as you do this more, reading tenants would be easier over time.

You can make use of a rental questionnaire that will surely help you learn if every prospective tenant is a great fit. You must, however, be sensitive about the things you will ask the applicants. You don't want to ask them about their personal lives, beliefs, and political preferences. In order to find a good tenant, you have to do the following:

- ❖ Know where they work and how much they earn

- ❖ Perform a background and credit check

- ❖ Ask for their references

- ❖ Call their former landlords

- ❖ Interview them face-to-to

Even though you do all of these things, you may miss something that specifies a bad tenant. Since screening tenants could be pretty tricky, it might be a good idea to hire a third-party tenant screening service that will help you analyse all gathered information to meet the best tenants.

Writing and Reviewing Rental Contracts

When you find a good tenant for your property, it is going to be time to sign the rental contract. If you have no idea how to make a contract, you can find existing contracts online that you can use as a reference.

Otherwise, you can always get help from a real estate agent or a lawyer that will make sure that you wouldn't be missing any details on the paper. From there, you are able to work by yourself. Don't forget to put details regarding rental payment schedule, maintenance information, eviction process, and home rules within the contract. Furthermore, you have to make sure that you disclose and gather a security deposit when you are the agreement.

Review the Contract

Reread the contract again before presenting it to the new tenant, and again, reread it together with the tenant. Make sure that the tenant reads and understands what's written on the contract. Also, give him a chance to ask questions, or if he has confusions, be ready to answer him clearly.

Walking Through the Property

Before making it official, you can have a final check on everything with your new tenant. Explain everything and document all the details you can possibly note.

With these details, you can be sure that you have proof that everything was well before the tenant came in. This is useful in case there are some sort of disagreements in the future over damages or other issues.

Step 4: Checking and Maintenance

Once the new tenant has moved into the property, you might think that you no longer have a responsibility over the property during the time of his stay. Well, this is not always the case if you're a responsible landlord. Because that property is still considered yours, you'll be the person to call in case a problem occurs. If something goes wrong with anything in the house, you'll be the one to fix it. For example, if the heater suddenly stops working, then you're the one responsible for getting it fixed.

Rental Visits

It's very beneficial to make a scheduled visit to the property at least every 6 months.

You can visit them after a few months of them staying in to make sure that there's no problem with the place. This will also make the tenant feel that you are open to hearing anything as some tenants tend to be too shy to disturb the landlord. There might be small problems popping up that they had not yet reported to you; these walkthroughs are the best time to get some more insight.

On top of seeing how they are doing, doing a visit also helps you make sure that your property is being respected by its tenants. By making the tenant know that you do regular visits to the property, they will be more likely to take care of the property even more.

Regular Maintenance

Every property requires some sort of maintenance. When small problems pop out, like plumbing or heater problems, your tenants will be more likely to contact you. And of course, they also expect you to take action immediately to fix them.

To do the maintenance faster, you must prepare yourself in advance:

- ❖ List of reliable local workers

- ❖ Contact information for local landlords who can help

- ❖ List of basic repair problems that you can fix your own

- ❖ Specific maintenance fund

- ❖ Set schedule for regular check-ups of appliances, especially the AC and heaters

Big Repairs

While all landlords hope that it wouldn't happen, there's always the chance that you'll have to take on a huge repair while you're getting the property rented out. There might be big problems that happen to the property. These problems might be due to natural disasters like flooding or tornado.

If the property requires an important repair that is going to force your tenant to get out of the property for a few days, it's your responsibility to give them housing during that period because they already paid. As the property owner, you should be responsible for where they are going to spend the nights while the property is being fixed, whether it means renting a hotel for them.

If ever something very serious happens to the house that it becomes impossible for anyone to live there, you have to talk to the tenant and tell them that the lease contract might have to be ended earlier. So, make sure to mention on your contract that in case of critical damage on the property due to damage caused by natural disaster or unforeseen event, the contract might get terminated.

Step 5: Collecting Rent

One of the most important jobs of a landlord is to collect the rent! Each landlord has a different preference for collecting rent. Some still pay in checks or some may use electronic banking or online payment systems like PayPal and Venmo.

Each method may come with its own pros and cons, but ultimately, it all depends on you which one you think is most convenient. If you choose the online system, however, you have to keep in mind that it might deduct some fee, so make sure to work this out with your tenant.

Raising Rent

Because of the rising expenses in the area, it might come to a point when you have to raise your rent. Although it might sound impossible to raise the rent while an existing tenant lives there, this thing happens more often than you think. So, in the contract, make sure to state the possibility of raising the rent. It's up to them whether they still want to stay at the property or look for somewhere else to live.

Late Fees

Make sure to apply a late fee for all the renters who didn't pay their dues on time. If the tenant is always late when paying their rents, make sure that they know the possibility of eviction if they keep resisting to pay on time.

Tenants are going to come up with all the excuses in the book for their late payments, and being empathetic about their situation is okay. However, when a tenant starts to consecutively pay their rent very late, it is a sign that they might no longer be able to afford your property.

By enforcing a clear policy regarding late fees, you are going to have peace of mind that they are going to avoid paying their rent late.

The late fees policy must be made clear in the rental agreement. Don't forget to include relevant parts of the contract as a reference when giving them the notice of late payment. It should be clear to them that possible eviction may happen.

Step 6: Evictions

No landlord ever wants to be in a position where they want to evict people, but this is something that happens constantly. As a new landlord, you probably don't have any idea what to do when you get into such a situation, and it's okay. To make sure that you're following the local laws, doing research beforehand would be necessary.

The eviction process might involve a whole court process if the tenant refuses to leave. The whole process can be a little bit frustrating, but it's very important to follow the legal process to avoid any possible trouble.

Any form of an attempt to evict the tenant yourself can be considered a criminal offence. In order to avoid trouble, here are some of the basic steps you may need to follow:

* Send them the official notice, which states the deadline until when they could fix the issue that breaches the agreement.

* If the conditions are not met, file the eviction with the court.

* When filing for eviction, don't accept any form of payment from the tenant. Doing so may invalidate the process of eviction.

* Be aware of the local laws to make sure that you're not breaking any rules.

* You may want to hire a lawyer if you find the law confusing.

* Wait for the court ruling and local sheriff to do the actual eviction.

Step 7: Accounting

Accounting and tax management is something that is very important, but you might not be good at it. Fortunately, you can always hire a property manager to help you. If you had a property management company, they're going to produce this information in reports for you, but doing it by yourself can be quite complicated.

To make the business accounting easier, here are some tips you may want to follow.

1. You can hire an accountant to do the taxing for you; the cost is worth it. They are going to help you maximize deductions and guarantee a clean record.

2. The money spent on maintenance and other basic property maintenance should be clearly documented.

3. To avoid confusion, you may want to have separate bank accounts for your business expenses.

4. Save money that will cover taxes and other fees that you may find surprising.

Becoming a Property Manager

Becoming a good rental manager is a responsibility you may want to master! While you can always hire someone to do this, doing it yourself will save you a lot of money. And after all, it's not that complicated.

Keep in mind that in its most minimalistic form, property management needs only some simple steps:

❖ Purchase and repair a property

❖ Set up rental expenses and tenant requirement

❖ Search for tenants and rent the house to them

❖ Maintain the property

❖ Collect rent and pay taxes

❖ Enjoy the profit!

Managing a property can be overwhelming, especially for beginners, but this shouldn't be the case. When done properly using the knowledge you acquire as you research on this field, you will be rewarded not only with monetary wealth but also with the satisfaction that you are able to manage such a complicated task.

9.1 Different Ways You Can Advertise Your Rental Property

Getting your rental filled is of main concern when you're turning over rental units. Landlords know that a vacant unit equals to lost profits. That's why having a good marketing strategy is so extremely important. Just filling the unit isn't enough; smart landlords see the marketing effort as the first step to screen the tenants. A good marketing campaign is the best method for landlords to lower the risk of picking the best person to rent the unit. They would like to make sure that the person they choose can pay rent on time and accomplish the responsibilities of the lease. Having to pick a marginal tenant due to lack of options can prove to be expensive. The cost evictions, turnover, maintenance, and repairs can be pretty overwhelming.

❖ The best and easiest means to advertise your rental home is the time-tested "For Rent" sign. As simple as it may look like, this means capitalizes on the idea that renters are going to drive around desired communities seeking future housing.

In order to improve visibility, it's recommended that a sign be placed on the property. A lot of landlords put a small box on one of the signs to place flyers with rental information. This will let the landlord disqualify prospects by revealing price, expectations, and policy. Qualifying prospects are going to save much time by cutting pointless showings and phone calls.

Signs should reveal contact information visibly and should be written in big print. A lot of landlords lose rental opportunities by making the writing extremely small or hard to read. Make sure that the sign will attract the eyes of everyone who will pass by. You can make it extra attractive by adding two balloons next to the sign.

❖ The second most efficient advertising method is to distribute the rental details flyer to every free community bulletin board in the area. You can find these boards at public places like churches, grocery stores, community centres, as well as government offices.

Be ready and put announcements or flyers about the availability of your rental property on bulletin boards in the area. This way is especially effective if you're marketing to college students and immigrants.

❖ Another effective way is asking people to endorse your rental property and giving them commission once they successfully find it. Customary referral rewards range from $50 to $200. This is effective and always works faster.

❖ Another classic yet effective way is making the most of classified ads in newspapers. They could be more expensive if you choose newspapers in most cities. However, you can simply choose a smaller local newspaper as they are cheaper. Ads in big newspapers are usually extremely short since word usage is limited. Smaller publications let more information in the ad.

❖ Now, for the most effective way of advertising – using online ads. Everyone is online now. You can put your ads on Facebook or Craigslist, and you'll surely be flooded with inquiries about your property. By using the internet, you don't have to worry about only adding limited words on the ads. You can write as many details as you want and you can also upload pictures in order for potential tenants to have a vision of what the unit looks like even without visiting the property in person.

9.2 How to Get the Best Tenants

Choosing a tenant can be a complicated process, but it doesn't have to be. There are landlords who tend to be relaxed about this process, and it's mostly because they've done this several times, and they already know that they are doing. Even though there's no sure-fire way for you to know everything about the tenant, there are several ways to have a better understanding of the tenant before you accept them to live in your property. Here are important things you must always remember.

Pay heed to the overall presentation of the possible tenant

Of course, every landlord should act in accordance with Fair Housing rules and laws. But then again, it's possible for landlords to consider the overall presentation of the potential tenant. The tenant's sex, age, or race doesn't have to do with it, but rather the overall presentation for the first impression such as the way they dress, talk, and carry themselves.

Perform a credit check

A credit check might require a fee on the part of the tenant or the owner, depending on which state they are in. A credit check is going to give a record of how the tenant has settled his previous financial responsibilities. This is going to include information about collections, late payments, and delinquencies. In today's age, the economy has been pretty unstable, so always keep in mind that if the prospective tenant has any type of financial problem. Most tenants usually have some kind of flaw, so don't expect anyone to be a perfect person. Actually, your main worry should be to know as to whether or not the tenant is able to pay his rent or not.

Perform a background check

A background check can be performed through an organization for a small fee, and it's definitely worth it. A background check usually involves checking of lawsuits, criminal record, and other public information that proves that the potential tenant is not a threat. Again, no one is perfect, and one flaw shouldn't make them disqualified to be your tenant. But if you see that they have recorded offences such as sexual assault, robbery, and domestic violence, then you should avoid accepting them.

Make a high-quality application as well as a lease agreement

You might want to ask help from a legal expert to create a professional and high-quality application and lease agreement. This document is crucial as it explains your expectations and your role as a landlord. This document is going to be your protection in case things go wrong with your tenant, so the little fee you might spend is definitely worth it.

Keep a fair screening process

As a landlord, it's important to keep a fair screening process for possible tenants. So, you have to make sure that every decision you make is based on business online and not any personal information. That's why I discourage landlords to ask their potential tenants about their religion, sexual orientation, political beliefs, and other things that could lead to disagreement.

Tenant interview

Doing a brief interview with a potential tenant is a good way to get to know them and know their needs and expectations. Don't say anything that could be interpreted as discrimination, but it's okay to ask about whether they have pets, how many people are going to stay in the unit, and whether they are a smoker or not.

The truth is that there's always a risk, and you cannot guarantee how the tenant will act when they finally move into your place. Only because a tenant looks a certain way, it doesn't mean that he's going to be a good or bad tenant. The best thing a landlord could do is use the options at their disposal such as background checks, credit checks, and interviews in order to develop a complete picture of the tenant before they move in.

9.3 How to Protect Yourself from Bad Tenants

Hoarding, late payments, unauthorized roommates, and illegal activities – tenant problems come in different sizes, shapes, and forms, and the severity differs from each other. Even with the most severe process of screening and property rules in place, if you're a landlord, you're likely to deal with these things at some point in your life. With any problems, however, being professional is a must and will definitely take you a long way: Communicate clearly and immediately, and take the important steps – regardless of how complicated they may be – to keep a safe and lucrative rental.

Now, in this subchapter, we're going to talk about the proper ways how you can handle common problems tenants face and lease violations they commit. The key to dealing with tenants that are pretty difficult is to document everything. Each state has different laws, so again, make sure to ask a legal professional for advice on what to do when a problem with tenants arises.

Okay, so you're having trouble with your tenant...

Perhaps, he's not paying the rent on time for the last few weeks. Or the neighbours have been contacting you that your tenants are making noise at late hours. Maybe complaints of loud music and foul smell have begun flooding in. It's best to set your emotions aside the moment you feel like a problem is starting to arise. When a problem arises, remember that there are only two possible outcomes – it's either the tenant fixes the problem, or he leaves. There are few things to remember before you get on justifying a problem with your tenant.

❖ Know the law

Every state follows its own laws and ordinances. As a landlord, it's your responsibility to know the laws, rights, and all the responsibilities that go with being a property owner. Again, if you need to know more, don't be afraid to contact an attorney.

❖ Follow the policies and processes

The moment the tenant signs the contract, it means that they are ready to follow your terms, rules, and policies in running the property. Ask the tenant if they have further questions regarding the rules you apply and give them the copy so they can read it again later on.

The lease agreement must explain what tenants are allowed and not allowed to do with the property, the amount they need to pay, when is it due, and how it is going to be paid. On top of it, it's important to include rules about noise, resident-to-resident argument resolution, landlord responsibilities, tenant responsibilities, guidelines on additional occupants, pets, guests, smoking, maintenance of the property, and normal deterioration.

❖ Document everything

As mentioned earlier, this is the most important thing you could do for yourself as a landlord. Document the policies and procedures for dealing with the problem or complaint of the tenant, which includes expected response times, types of communication, notices, warnings, and when to escalate the problem. Sometimes, a meeting is needed where you can discuss the incident reports and perform incident reviews with your team in a meeting. You might also want to make incident reports and conduct incident review meetings with the tenants and your team.

❖ Get training

If you hire a staff to help you manage your business, then you have to make sure they are fully familiar with the whole processes and policies, that know your policies and procedures, and that they know the different types of tenant warnings, termination notices, as well as incident reports. When the tenant is emotional, getting fired up is an easy thing as well. And no matter how disrespectful a tenant might be, keeping professionalism is something each of the members must practice all the time.

A respectful conversation with the tenant might be enough to stop the problem before it escalates. If ever a non-legal problem happens, you can call the tenant and ask if you can meet in person to discuss and fix the problem. Use your judgment because there are cases when help from the authorities might be needed. Be specific and direct when it comes to your discussion and highlight the problem and the consequences of not following the policies and rules. Rather than saying, "Let me know when you'll remove the trash," say, "Get rid of the trash by Sunday, otherwise, you'll have to pay a fine." By having a basic knowledge of these techniques and strategies, it's going to be easier for you to navigate a solution to the problem a tenant might be having.

❖ It is not personal, so it shouldn't be

As a landlord, it's possible for you to deal with tenants with some heart-breaking stories. It's okay to be understanding, but all in all, you must be firm and solid when it comes to sticking to your policies. You have these policies to protect you and your business. On top of it, this type of discussion should only be discussed between you and the tenant. Significant others or family members may want to get involved, but this should only be between you and your tenant.

❖ Treat your tenant with respect

There are some problems that are not easy to discuss with your tenant – some of these are late payment and hoarding. See to it that you treat problems with privacy, even though they are not technically confidential data. Be careful when sharing sensitive information with people who shouldn't be involved. Furthermore, if you set a schedule to meet up with the tenant to discuss something, make sure to show up there on time.

❖ Put safety first

If it happens that a certain situation is already putting anyone in danger, then don't wait and call the police right away. Although you want to apply professionalism at all times, you shouldn't risk anyone's safety in exchange for anything. Call the authorities right away when you suspect that your tenant is involved in anything illegal. When criminal charges are pressed, you can then carry on with eviction process.

❖ Notice of termination

As a landlord, you can use several kinds of warnings and notices. Familiarize yourself with the local laws to see how you can serve the notice, particularly when it is an eviction notice, and ensure that you are serving the right notice to deal with the issue.

These are 3 of the most common notices:

- ❖ **Non-payment of Rent Notice:** Use this in case a tenant fails to pay rent on time. It notifies the tenants to settle their payment within a specified amount of time, or they will be forcedly evicted.

- ❖ **Quit Notice:** This is used when a tenant violates a term or condition of the lease. The tenant should have a specific amount of time to fix the problem, or they are going to be forcedly evicted.

- ❖ **Vacate Notice:** This is used when a tenant causes serious, recurrent, or dangerous acts. The tenant doesn't have a chance to fix anything, and they need to leave.

Each of these notices must include these basic elements for them to be valid. Here are the specifics you may want to include when sending a notice:

- ❖ **The name and address of the tenant**

- ❖ **Information about the violation**

- ❖ **The number of days wherein the tenant should comply**

- ❖ **Signature and date**

Chapter 10

REAL ESTATE TAX & LEGALITIES

Every state in the US maintains a tax assessor's office. So, what is the tax assessor? This office is responsible for evaluating the value of all real estate set in the county. This is also the one that is responsible for keeping precise records of location and ownership. The tax assessor makes an assessment of a particular property, enters the assessment into the records and takes up or takes down the property tax by how much the price has gone up or went down. The office of the treasurer is going to collect the taxes, but the tax assessor is responsible for putting up the rate.

Property taxes can go up or go down based on two different variables: the amount owed and the rate. Tax rates that are going up but falling property values may lead to a lesser or greater amount owed. At the same time, rising property values and falling tax rates could have an equally indeterminate result when it comes to how much the homeowner needs to pay. The worst situation is a rising tax rate and rising property value. All in all, these taxes are one of the most troublesome features of homeownership. Homeowners should be mindful of the things they are able to do to raise or lower their taxes on the property.

A definite way to bring up the property tax amount owed is to add value to the property. Home improvement, cleaning up the yard, improving the looks of the curb, repainting the walls, just anything that could raise the value of the property can raise its tax liability. The fastest way to avoid this is just don't build. Alternatively, if a structural or cosmetic improvement should be made, the homeowner could consult the tax assessor's office beforehand.

A very simple way to lower property tax assessments is to go to assessor's office and ask for a copy of the property tax record. Mistakes, however, are very common. If you see a mistake on the record, the assessor has to, by law, make it right. Sometimes a whole re-evaluation may be in order, as mistakes on the part of the assessor can cost homeowners a lot in taxes.

Assessed values depend greatly on the home's exterior attractiveness. The appeal of the curb then plays a big role in the tax assessment. The tax assessor has many scopes when considering improvements to external features. Again, the best way to avoid this is to not to make improvements until the assessment is done. Or just don't do them at all if possible.

Make sure to let the assessor in whenever he wants to perform the assessment. If you deny him entrance, it may give him complete freedom to put the highest value possible to your property – so be nice. Unfortunately, this unconditional authority happens in most states in the United States.

10.1 How to Calculate Property Taxes

One of the most confusing things you might have to deal with as a real estate investor is calculating the taxes. But then again, this is something anyone can learn. This is especially the fact because even though calculations aren't always the same for all local governments, the same rules are normally followed.

The Assessment of the Property

The local tax assessor's office is the one who is going to determine the value of your property. Usually, this assessment is done annually or after every few years. This all depends on the law of the state or municipality. Before you can get your property tax bills, you are required to get value assessment first.

The assessment is derived from the estimation of the tax assessor based on the property's market value. The value may come in three different forms:

❖ **The cost method:** This is when the assessor calculates the total amount of the property if it was to be built from scratch. Of course, this varies based on how old the house is and where it is located.

❖ **Sales comparison:** The assessor will base the value of your property on other properties of the same type, size, and condition, located in the same area or town. He'll then adjust for variables that might make your property more or less valuable compared to others that were sold.

❖ **The income method:** This assessment is usually used in business and commercial properties. Here, the possible amount of income if the property were to be rented out is calculated.

Chapter 11

BUILDING AN ESSENTIAL TEAM

Building a real estate investing team is important in achieving massive success in real estate investments. Many of the best real estate investors are aware of the real value that a team could add. After all, it's going to be too difficult, if not, impossible, for you to do everything by yourself. And this is where the investing team comes into the picture.

What Is A Real Estate Investing Team?

A real estate investing team is a group of experts with whom to work closely with before, during, and after purchasing real estate investments. The real estate investing team helps with financing, sourcing deals, the process of due diligence, and dealing with your real estate investments. As you start building your real estate portfolio, having a reputable team can help you save a lot of time, resources, and money. The secret to building a successful team is to find reliable people to depend on. Build a reliable team of experts that you trust.

What Is the Purpose of this Team?

A complete team for your real estate business guide requires mentioning the value of building a successful real estate team. Each person has different real estate goals and ambitions, but no matter what yours are, you stand a better chance of attaining them with the help of your core team members. You must see your real estate investing team members as business partners that are important to helping you attain greater success in your real estate investing endeavour.

Who Are the Main Members of a Real Estate Investing Team?

Here are the members that make a great team. Let's look at each of them to better understand their role and purposes.

1. Spouse or Significant Other

Your spouse or that special someone plays a significant role in the success of your real estate investing journey. Having someone who you know will be on the same page with you all the time can help you emotionally in keeping yourself on track. The main reason as to why you need someone who is always on the same page with you is that this person has a big impact on life, and this person impacts the way you manage your funds, make your decisions, and work on your thoughts and ambitions.

2. Real Estate Agents

A real estate agent is another key member that will make your team strong and efficient. A reliable real estate agent can help you find the best deals available and put a bid on your behalf. He is familiar with the marketplace and knows how to do transactions. Real estate agents are able to act on behalf of the seller or buyer. Usually, real estate agents earn money by commission by the seller of a property. So, if you're thinking about adding a real estate agent to be in your team to help you purchase a property, this is going to be free. However, you have to make sure that you're not working with just any real estate agent. As much as possible, look for someone who really knows a thing or two about investing and has experience about it.

3. LENDERS

Forming strong relationships with conventional and private money lenders is a smart move for any real estate investor. Lenders could range from small community banks to credit unions to bigger commercial banks. Mortgage brokers and mortgage firms are also smart options. If those options are not enough, you can go with private or hard money lenders. No matter which path you decide to take on or when you choose to take it, the important thing is to build relationships with different lenders. Start to build relationships with these lenders now, so once a good opportunity comes, and it will, you will be ready with the right financing.

4. Contractors and Handymen

Having contractors and handymen in your team to deal with repairs is important for your real estate business. In order to find these people, you may ask for referrals from other real estate investors, or you can also find them online. Don't forget to check their references. Ask the contractor's references if they showed up on schedule and finished the work on time. Are they trustworthy? Did they do the job well? Are they trustworthy? Furthermore, you have to remember that the cheapest option may not be the best option. It might take some deep searching to find the perfect contractor, so being patient is important. You have to keep in mind that your goal is to build a team that can truly help you with your business.

5. Bookkeeper

You might want to have a bookkeeper in your team to help keep a good and accurate record of outgoing debits and incoming credits in the company. A bookkeeper could help you track all the expenses and income you can, and help prepare your finances throughout the tax season. An accurate account of income and expenses is important, and as you begin to generate more wealth and have more properties to manage, a reliable bookkeeper can be really beneficial for your business.

6. Accountant

Having a certified public accountant or CPA to your real estate team is also a very smart decision. A CPA can take the responsibility of preparing your personal and business tax returns, and on top of that, you can offer you solid advice when it comes to tax recommendations. Search for an accountant who has worked with other real estate experts or who knows a lot about real estate. Search for this team member as soon as possible, since a good CPA could help you pick the best tax-saving strategy for real estate investment.

7. Lawyer

A lawyer is an important part of any real estate team. A good lawyer can help draft and perform legally binding leases as well as other real estate documentation. Try to search for a lawyer that knows real estate or has worked with real estate investors in the past. A real estate lawyer could help you choose and set up the best legal article for managing your real estate properties.

8. Property Manager

The last but definitely not least is a property manager. From screening the tenants to making sure everything in order in the property itself, a property manager can help relieve you from some of the most time consuming and arduous tasks. This is something you want to look for once you have a fair amount of cash flow coming in and want your empire running as passive as it possibly can be. Do a thorough search in order to find a great property manager, and remember to check references.

WHEN SHOULD YOU BUILD YOUR REAL ESTATE INVESTING TEAM?

You must start your real estate investing team as soon as you can. The value your team increases as you make your professional relationship. These people are your teammates, and being aware of these key individuals as early as possible can help you attain success faster. Your real estate team could help throughout the due diligence period before even buying the property.

Chapter 12

Scaling Your Real Estate Empire

For many investors, closing a couple of deals automatically means success. Maybe they've found a couple of great units and started getting them rented out. Or maybe you could add a house a year to your rental properties. But still, after starting off well on your business, it might still hit a plateau. And the fundamental difference between growing and scaling a business is one of the main reasons as to why this is the case.

The skills needed to grow a business and how to scale it actually vary. Your ability to grow your business usually depends just on your hustle and knowledge. In terms of scaling a business, it is a whole different ballpark.

With scaling, you're creating a foundation that gives you a room to grow and develop your business in future. If your goal is to expand your business by 100%, then you must prepare yourself to give your 100% as well. It always seems like 24 hours in a day are not enough for you to do everything you need to do. One of the best things to do is to search for ways how you can grow your small business into a big one by working smarter rather than working harder.

And to scale your real estate investment business properly, here are some methods you can follow.

- **Choose a niche**

"Shiny object syndrome" is a common condition that many entrepreneurs acquire. When you start mastering something, there is a chance a tendency for it to be quite a boring routine. As a businessman, this is something you need to avoid.

And to successfully evade this situation, there are three things you have to answer when you're in the business of real estate investment – or just about any kind of business.

The questions are:

❖ What's your passion?

❖ What can your organization do that is better than the competition?

❖ How good it is when it comes to generating revenue?

Once you have answered this question, find out the most relevant niche to the set of answers you come up with.

You can't find a lot of market segments like this for most companies. Keep in mind that it's hard to focus on different types of the market at the same time – it's possible but almost unbearable. For example, if your company focuses on buying and flipping real estate in working to middle-class areas, it's not going be very smart to get involved with low-income housing or luxury housing without making a very well-organized plan. If you can scale your business, it's going to be easy for you to focus! You may be familiar with different types of real estate investments, but don't expect to be an expert on any of them.

- **Create a Brain Trust**

In running a business, and searching for the right team to help you, the secret is to find and hire people that are smarter than you. It doesn't matter how smart you are; being good at everything is just too draining. This might involve requiring finding partners, searching for mentors, or forming a "mastermind group," but it's very important to search for people who can do everything you can and more.

Of course, putting it on the backburner is very easy, but you have to make a point to prioritize it as a part of the routine. And you will want to have more people to help you with your venture as your business expands.

- **Delegate**

As stated above, working harder is not enough to make your business work and grow. We only have 24 hours in a day, and they are not enough for everything we want and need to do. So, in order for you to manage your tasks better, you must learn how to delegate.

Economists have this term called "opportunity cost", which refers to when an investor or business misses out on something when picking out one alternative over another. In other words, when you're doing one thing at the moment, it means you're missing out something else. Always remember that time is money, so you have to make the most of it. And the best way to do that is to learn how to delegate.

Before hiring a single employee, you are able to delegate tasks to realtors, accountants, lawyer, property managers, and anyone on your team. You can even hire an assistant to help you do simple tasks for you that even though you know you can do yourself, it is much better if you do something else more profitable and beneficial for you in the long run. And automating as many things as possible becomes easier. And once you know that you're ready, you can delegate more tasks and responsibilities to more employees.

Doing this thing will help you free up your time and get the money faster. The delegation also offers what we have known as "intrinsic motivation" to the employees. Having sovereignty is a real motivator for people while being controlled can sap the motivation of any.

- **Trust, but verify**

Of course, with delegation comes a catch. You can always guarantee for people you delegate to actually do the job that is assigned to them. Realtors, assistants, contractors, and just about anyone else can also waste your money without giving you something valuable to your organization.

But there's something you can do to prevent this, which is to *measure*. Measuring, however, doesn't only go for more than only the performance of the employee. For all rehabs, make sure to always compare the actual expenses to the budget, even though it didn't go well and looking at it can be quite scary. By not looking at it carefully, you wouldn't know what's wrong, and you wouldn't know how to improve it.

For any of your employees, you must strive to make KPI or Key Performance Indicators. Every employee must be assigned to do specific tasks and cover a certain area of focus. And there has to key numbers that will measure their performance. Always take proper precautions on this, though. A real estate agent who just does most of the most complicated tasks might find it hard to finish all the tasks he needed to do. That's why it's a good idea to have some KPIs for all the positions and watch out for the confounding factors.

- **Standardize**

Figure out what renovations are going to add the most value to your investment properties derived from the return on investment, property type, comps, location, as well as other factors. Then, you may want to apply the same set of rehabilitations on each of the properties. For example, if your company uses the same interior paint, furniture, carpet, and blinds most of the rental units or units you sell, you may want to use a different colour, but use the same brand. You can stick to several colours and may switch up every so often, but as much as possible, you may want to use standardized brands.

All in all, scaling a business is deeper than how it can be seen from the outside. Keep in mind that these processes will let you grow your real estate business quicker than you could have possibly imagined, and you can do it easier as well. Similar to a house, a business couldn't be built without foundation.

12.1 Most Cost-Effective Strategies and Ways to Grow Your Businesses

The real estate market has been extremely robust, giving a lot of investors a great opportunity to increase sales transactions and earn a lot more income than they did many years ago.

Of course, there's no denying that technology has played a huge role in this growth in the real estate market. If your goal is to master this craft or at least prepare yourself to easily adapt in the industry, here are some ways you can follow to your make your business successful and make it grow.

1. Invest for appreciation

Improving investment properties with predictable appreciation down the line in order to generate better returns is the best strategy to develop a business. However, you must keep in mind that putting an investment for appreciation is a long-term approach doesn't guarantee that you will get good cash flow returns right away. But many smart investors choose to invest exclusively for appreciation. These people see the financial rewards overtime contrasted with the immediate cash fixes ones who choose to go short term get. If you invest exclusively for appreciation, know that this is riskier compared to investing for cash flow, but the ROI is much better.

2. Maximize positive cash flow properties

One of the best strategies you can follow to grow your business is to find positive cash flow properties. In other words, positive cash flow properties reap investors an excess of cash returns and cover the costs of owning the property altogether.

3. Utilize home equity to purchase more real estate

Another smart approach that we have previously mentioned in this book is to jumpstart your real estate investing through your home equity. If you're in a financial restraint, you may want to consider the use of your home equity as leverage to purchase real estate. This method will also save you money, and it doesn't require you to lean down backwards to pay the deposit straight from your own pocket.

4. Expand your real estate portfolio

Expanding is something you may learn to do. This is because by doing this, you increase your returns and at the same time, minimalizing the overall risk. If you want to be successful in this, you must learn how to expand and seek profitable real estate opportunities the best you can.

5. Renovate the property for maximum economic benefits

Renovation or home improvement, as mentioned in the earlier part of this book, is an important thing to do if you want to increase the value of the property, may it be for rental or selling purpose. The advice I want to give you is to learn how to recognize and prioritize work in the property that will provide you with the most benefits. This means you don't have to do renovations on it all at the same time. Instead, choose an area you think will be noticed by the potential buyer or tenant right away and fix it, then worry about the other parts later on.

6. Assign a Property Manager if needed

If managing daily operation has become overwhelming for you, then it's going to make more sense to get help from a professional who will be more than willing to help you run your business and keep your costs to a minimum. Hiring good property management can help you get a better ROI. This is especially the case if you have invested in multiple real estate properties.

All in all, being successful in this business involves business planning. This will help you maximize returns and giving you a business that will you lead you to financial freedom. Plan well and choose the best real estate growth strategy alongside your visions and financial objectives. Keep in mind that most successful real estate investors started off small and eventually worked their way up to win big.

CONCLUSION

Real estate offers many investment opportunities to anyone who is willing to try it. Generally, a lot of money might be required to get into this kind of business. Building your cash savings and reserves is necessary. While you're unlikely to risk your whole life savings if you make an investment in this field, but it's important to educate yourself. The return goes up in time and doesn't diminish if you know how to invest wisely.

As you can tell from this book, investing in real estate is one of the most complicated business activities you can do, but at the same time, it is rewarding in the long run. The truth is, this is a renowned investment vehicle particularly for the middle and upper class. Most people who have tried investing in real-estate have found this extremely rewarding even though it involves a lot of risks and effort.

Investing in this business is something that you must think about very carefully. Don't just get yourself into it unless you're 100% sure that you can handle it. But no matter how complicated it may seem, remember that this is something that anyone can learn with a great amount of dedication.

You must be aware that if you are new to this, you may face a lot of surprises, especially in the first part, which is the purchasing of the property. At first, you must determine what type of property investment you want to make before even looking for a house. Some of the most common investment property sources that you might consider include real estate agents, foreclosure sales, multiple listing services, and private sales.

You can find different ways to earn money from real estate you invested in. You might have it rented or appreciate its value by building equity. These are types of investments that can appreciate in value, and the property could provide you with an amazing increase in earnings after some years if done well. While real estate can generate long term income, as an investor, you must ask for advice from an experienced person or an expert who you know can develop and deliver an effective strategy from experience.

THE DIVIDEND INVESTING BLUEPRINT

BY

DALE WALTON

INTRODUCTION

A lot of the time, quite a number of people seem to get themselves worked up on how to boost their finances. Many people want to break free from "not having enough money" but they just simply don't have the knowledge on how to go about it. According to a study, the issue of not being financially buoyant has led quite a number of people to depression.

Has this ever been a problem you've had before? Well if it is, don't worry. Many people have been in your shoes, just sit back, relax, and enjoy the financial enlightenment this book will provide you with.

In this book, I'll explain all you need to know about having a money mindset, how to say goodbye to lack of money, and also the exact steps and strategies to get started investing in dividends.

I've written this book to help you understand how to be a good investor, how to avoid the pitfalls people fall into, and how to build that passive income we all dream of.

My father never knew the secrets behind investing until he had just ten years to retire. He kept saying he wished he had known earlier. My father has lived with this regret all his life despite making good use of this secret regardless of the time he discovered it. He practically lives large as a retiree right now (6 years after retirement) without having to sweat or work anymore.

You will understand the beauty of investing in dividends as well as the essential things you need to know about creating multiple streams of income. Our major focus in this book is investing in dividends. So many times, a lot of people work so hard, craving a lot of money yet earning very little. It took me several years to finally discover that what sets the rich apart from the poor actually lives in their mind and mentality.

I once told a man to ensure his next generation starts saving as early as 10 and he just didn't understand where I was coming from until I had shared some of these "financial truths" with him.

If your aim in life is to work really hard and continue to work until you are above eighty and old and wrinkled, leaving your family with nothing but your payslips to live with when you are gone, please do not read this book. However, if your desire is to leave your family a legacy when you are gone and ticking off your bucket list while you are retired, this book is for you.

There's a feeling of fulfillment that comes with living off all you worked hard for, while you are retired and no longer working. The feeling that comes with having your investments work for you is simply unbeatable.

While you may not end up having your name on Forbes list as the richest man on the planet, having the key to success as well as being a successful investor would definitely earn you much more than "money". How about the respect that comes with being an "investment guru?". For certain reasons, if you crave real success, you have to read this book.

The millennial generation doesn't seem to be interested in investing and as much as we think the act of investing is fading away, thousands of people are still earning loads of money from investing. It's never too late to step up your game and become the next most successful investor.

You will find in this book all the latest information you need to know about dividend investing as well as relevant information discovered from personal experiences of successful investors which would definitely help you make only the best decisions. Some people have failed several times while trying to invest; the personal experiences of these people have been compiled to let you know the kind of things you shouldn't do as an investor.

One of the numerous things you have to look forward to learning is the power of compounding; how to make a real profit from compounding, how companies pay dividends, how to understand a perfect pay-out ratio, how long you should hold stocks as well as the general misconceptions about dividends.

You will also learn the crucial terminologies and language of investing and the stock market, and how investing goes beyond something that can be understood without in-depth understanding.

This book is designed and written to prepare you towards every obstacle you might come across in the investing world. Failure to read this beginner-friendly book would cost you more damage than you could imagine as you might never learn the right way to invest and also never come across these "secrets to building your finances".

I have personally applied the tips in this book, and I must say that although I have made certain mistakes in life as an investor and lost a lot of money on poor investments through lack of education, my financial security and status have never been better.

Chapter 1

BECOMING FINANCIALLY AWARE

In this chapter, you will learn how to become financially aware. Quite a number of people do not feel the need to invest, because they have little to no knowledge of how to increase their finances and up their financial game. What do I mean by this? Financial awareness will liberate you from poverty.

If you think you are wealthy but have no knowledge about the secret to financial freedom, your wealth would definitely not last a lifetime. Do not be surprised, this is simply because people who have genuine wealth and those who are successful with money do not enjoy spending money; they enjoy making it. If you do not understand this and happen to be a spendthrift or you always find yourself exceeding your budget and going beyond your financial limits, you need to read on. Now, it doesn't matter how many financial errors you have made or how many regrets you have, this chapter will help you rectify every error and prepare you to become really better at investing.

At the end of this chapter, you would have known the difference between having an active income and the need to build a passive income through investing in reasonable assets.

The truth about investing is that those who got the idea of investing earlier have one regret in life. What regret do you think they have? Well, the only regret they have is "not starting earlier". What this tells you is, it's never too early to start investing, you are not too young to understand what the world of investment looks like and how to go about it the perfect way. A lot of people need answers to this golden question:

Why should we Invest? There are lots of reasons you ought to invest. However, you might be wondering if *investing* and *saving* mean the same thing. Well, let's try to clarify that. Saving and investing are two entirely different things, although a lot of people try to substitute them with each other and often mistake the two for the same thing. Investing can be defined according to Wikipedia as, the act of allocating money in the expectation of some benefit in the future. In other words, it can be defined as an act of growing your money or making your money appreciate while setting it aside for future purposes.

Now, what is **SAVING?** A lot of economists believe that saving is simply the act of spending less in the present, in order to spend abundantly in the future. Saving can further be defined as the act of putting aside an amount of money which you do not have plans for at the moment, for emergencies, or for a future purpose.

The difference between saving and investing is that the money you set aside to save has to be an amount of money you want to be able to access quickly with little or no risk, and with a very little amount of taxes.

You might keep a particular amount of money in your piggy bank, under your mattress, or somewhere in your apartment. Such money can also be kept in a financial institution for a certain period of time, which is mostly a short time. This is because you do not have plans to spend the money at the moment but would like to reach such money easily when an emergency calls for it, or when the need arises.

On the other hand, investing basically means the act of acquiring assets such as stocks, mutual funds, or real estate, with the prospect of making money from such investments in the nearest future. Most investments are made for the sole purpose of achieving long-term goals. Now that you know the difference between investing and saving, you should understand the benefits of investing.

WHY DO YOU NEED TO INVEST AND GROW YOUR MONEY?

We all need money for our day-to-day activities. Money is an essential part of human life and just like human life itself, you need to grow your money. The very moment a person stops growing is the moment such a person stops existing. If you fail to grow your finances, the death of your financial life is certain.

A lot of millionaires and billionaires wake up every day to think of how to multiply their money, how to expand their finances, and invest in more business opportunities. I will tell you the story of a young man who inherited a whooping sum of money. This young man was richer than the head of state at that time and was envied by all. The only mistake he made was relying on this cash he had at hand; he got himself more liabilities than assets. He had a fleet of modern cars which required regular maintenance. He also slept in five-star hotels, and within two years, guess what happened? The money was gone in no time at all.

The point here is, it doesn't matter how much or how little you have, it's certain you can improve your financial status if only, you would master the art of investing. The good news is that successful investors didn't wake up one morning to become successful; they practiced the art of investing and became experts. You can become an excellent investor as well.

One mistake a lot of people make with money is believing in the current value of money, without considering how the rate of inflation can rise beyond the current value of your money. Also, It's high time we stopped depending on the government. One reason you need to start investing now is that the government might just go bankrupt if nobody decides to grow their own money.

Other reasons you need to invest and grow your money are as follows:

❖ **To earn an amazing return:** A lot of people invest their money in order to earn an amazing return. This basically means that one of the reasons for investing money is to gain something higher than your initial capital. You have to invest your money in a place where you can get a high rate in return. When there is an increase in your return, you will most definitely earn more money as well. Unlike saving, investing your money provides an opportunity to earn higher rates of return as well as interest. Therefore, if you would like to get a higher return on your money, it is advisable to invest such money instead of saving it.

❖ **To create a legacy:** It is the onus of a responsible parent to create a legacy for his/her children and family. One reason you need to invest your money in assets is to create a legacy when you leave. The last thing you want is to leave your family to suffer when something happens in the future. One amazing way to leave a legacy behind you is to start investing for the future when you are still young, agile, and able. A lot of people who have done this in the past have made their family happy while others who didn't feel the need to save when they were younger often grow up into old people who regret not making the decision of investing while they were younger. There are different options out there such as estates, stocks, shares, and mutual funds, which would definitely appreciate in the future and earn more money.

❖ Retirement: **Why should you save for retirement?** Retirement is an inevitable part of human life. It is the period you have to step down from work or give up on work. Whether we like it or not, the truth is that the human body isn't designed to work forever; this is as a result of declining skills, health, and other factors that come with old age. This period is a crucial part of your life and a huge reason you should take the issue of investing seriously. One reason why you should invest for retirement is to sit back and make your money "work" for you. Before retirement, you'd have spent so many years working around the clock in order to make money; post-retirement should, therefore, be a time when all the money accumulated over the years should do the "work" for you. It is indeed a time you should sit back and enjoy your hard-earned money. While it is believed that retirement is meant for old and inactive people, a lot of people have broken this myth by retiring early after investing enough money for their retirement. It is indeed an achievement to retire at 40 or below such age. A certain man named Jeremy Jackson retired at the age of 38 after saving up fifty percent of his income for ten years. Another man named Todd Tresidder also retired at the age of 35 after investing for 12 years. It's not impossible for you to retire early, as long as you imbibe the culture of investing. The story of these early successful retirees tells you that you need to start investing for the sake of retirement if you do not want to run out of money in the future. Everyone has certain expectations in life, one of such expectations is having a bucket list. Some people also happen to have exotic dreams in life. Sometimes you want to explore what the world looks like, visit iconic places, purchase certain things in life and so on. Almost everyone would like the thought of having a vacation in Paris, while cruising in a yacht with champagne in your hand and a big smile on your face; living your best life, off your investments without working for a dime anymore. The best time to do these things you have always wanted to do and also tick off your bucket list is after retirement. In order to have this life you have always wanted, you need to start investing when you are young, to have something to fall back on, retire early, and also live a fancy life after retirement. One other reason you should invest for the purpose of retirement is to ensure that you do not become a burden on your loved ones after retirement. It is not a good idea to live your post-retirement life, depending on your family for survival. While this would earn you less respect, it might also not provide you the kind of life you have always wanted as the rest of your life would be spent depending on people for survival. You can also save yourself from going to an early grave, if you choose to invest for the purpose of retirement as failure to do this might just make you continue working and stressing yourself when you are grey and old. This is the period you should be resting and not working as any work you do at this stage of your life may cause your health to deteriorate and confine you to the sick bed for the rest of your life. A lot of health problems also come with old age; it is the reason you should invest in assets in case of emergencies in the future. You might also need to provide for your family after retirement. Since no pension can replace your salary, the best way to provide your family with a good life after retirement is to invest and make a living, off your investments. Finally, retirement should be the best time of your life; you would not be working for a very long time. Not having enough money can lead you to depression and frustration. The only way to save yourself from such is to invest for the future while you are still working.

❖ **Establish a business:** For some people, the purpose of investing is to establish a business, venture into new businesses, or develop an existing business. You can choose to invest in order to support a growing business or establish your own business. It is never wrong to have more than one source of income. Having multiple sources of income, on the other hand, will help you become financially stable. Investing in small businesses also affords you the opportunity to buy an ownership stake. While investing in other people's businesses can earn your financial freedom, it also helps you impact other people's lives as well.

❖ **Urgent funds:** One important reason you should invest is for the purpose of urgent or emergency funding. You never know what's going to happen the next minute. A lot of people have experienced unexpected/unforeseen events and circumstances such as a sudden layoff or setback from work. While it is good to be optimistic, you also need to prepare for the worst, just in case something unexpected happens to you or someone close to you. When such a situation arises, the best way to handle it is to have an emergency fund, which is one reason a lot of people invest. People invest for emergency purpose in order to save themselves from job loss, medical or dental emergency, unexpected home repairs, car maintenance, and unplanned vacation expenses. Although a lot of people do not feel any need to invest their emergency fund, one benefit you can earn is to hypothetically increase your net worth. Investing for emergency purpose will definitely save you from unnecessary stress as you can always have something to depend on when life brings something unexpected your way.

❖ **Time value of money**: When people invest, sometimes the only reason is "time value of money". What do I mean by this? The concept of time value in finance simply means that $1000 at hand is worth more than the equivalent amount in the nearest future. This is simply because investing $1000 will definitely earn you much more in the future. The sooner you invest your money, the sooner it works for you because a thousand dollar now might lose the value it has, when acquired in the next few years. The main idea behind the concept of the time value of money simply means you need to invest now rather than later so as to grow your money over time and to also enjoy a long term compound interest.

Now that you already know the value of investing and the importance of investing, the next question is how much you should invest? "I want to invest but I'm confused about how to start and how much I need to begin with". If this is you, you have no cause to be worried. Although, there is no fixed amount to be invested as you need to do something convenient for you and not go beyond your limits. You should only invest an amount of money that won't stop you from sleeping at night. Only what you can afford to lose should be invested as you do not want to end up in the hospital when something unexpected happens. One great way to start investing is to start with the same amount you would usually save up monthly. If you are used to saving 20% of your income monthly, you might just decide to invest exactly the same amount monthly. However, I personally think that making a decision to invest has a lot to do with how much responsibilities you have, the amount of money you would invest if you were single would be totally different from the amount you would invest if you were married. The kind of goals you also want to reach in life and the time you plan to achieve such goals should also determine how much you would invest. For instance, if you plan to retire early (at a certain age), you need to invest more (a certain percent of your income) and spend less in order to reach your goal faster. Think of the kind of goals you have. Your goal might be to pay for your offspring's college education. If this is your goal, you need to know how much time you have before your child goes to college and invest towards this time by approximating a rational rate of return for your investment assortment. You can work towards this goal by investing just enough money every month. Calculating how much you need to save becomes really easy when your goals are defined and specific. There are also various calculators you can find online if you need to figure out exactly how much money you should set aside to reach your goal. If you also have the money you aren't using at the moment or any idle money you do not see yourself spending in the next few years, such money should be invested, as it would increase over time. The general idea about investing is to check your financial life. Once you are able to meet your goals and you have settled "every bill", the next thing is to invest everything you have to spare. Investing also depends on how much tax an individual pays; people who earn a lower income are expected to substitute an increased percent of their salary than folks who earn a higher income. This is because they are required to pay less tax and it isn't pragmatic to cut down if you are already on the breadline.

DIVERSIFYING OF INCOME

After understanding the importance of investing and what percentage of your income you need to invest, one other important concept you should understand is the importance of diversifying your income. Income diversification has to do with coming up with various revenue streams that are independent of each other. Diversification is a procedure that condenses risk by apportioning investments among numerous financial instruments, industries, and other classifications. It targets to capitalize on returns by investing in several areas that would each react contrarily to the same event. Several investment practitioners believe that although it does not guarantee against loss, diversification is the utmost essential component of attaining long-term monetary goals while abating risk. Our aim here is to explore the truth behind this and why you need to achieve diversification in your portfolio. Investors are often confronted with two focal kinds of risk when investing. The primary is undiversifiable, which is also the same as systematic or market risk. Every company is associated and connected with this kind of risk. This type of risk is often caused by an increase in inflation rates, exchange rate, political insecurity, war, and changes in interest rates. This type of risk is not actually particular to a specified company or industry, and such risks can never be eradicated or jettisoned through diversification. However, it is one kind of risk investors have to deal with.

The entire stock market is generally affected by systematic risk, not just a particular investment vehicle or industry is affected.

The subsequent kind of risk is diversifiable. This risk is also the same as unsystematic risk and is explicit to a company, industry, market, economy, or country. It can be reduced through diversification. The most rampant sources of unsystematic risk are business risk and monetary risk. Consequently, the aim of diversifying is to invest in several assets in order to avoid getting everything affected the same way by market happenings. Diversification also has a lot to do with going beyond your own geographical locations to source for several investment opportunities. Subsequently, the stocks and bonds in Europe may not be affected by volatility in the United States. This means investing in that part of the world may curtail and reduce the risks of investing in your own geographical location.

The concept of income diversification isn't a luxury or privilege; it is a necessity for everyone who has an intelligent attitude towards his/her finances. What is the concept of diversifying income? The concept of diversifying income simply means you need to have more than one source of income. In other words, it is basically the act of learning not to put all your eggs in a basket. Although, we sometimes get really comfortable with our income in life to the extent that we do not feel the need to diversify or have more than one income stream, this attitude of being really secure about your sense of income isn't the best. This is not about being pessimistic or expecting the worst to happen, it is, on the other hand, being financially alert and prepared for the worst. What am I trying to say here? I'm saying, no matter how fulfilling your job is, or how big your salary is, you need to have a side hustle or a side business just in case something unexpected happens. There are several ways you could work toward creating multiple streams of income. You might decide to set an hour or more than an hour each day in order to push for new sales, brainstorm about the kind of business you want to venture in asides from what you are doing presently. Look around you to see if there's any kind of service lacking in your environment or office and work towards providing such services. Don't be scared of attempting a new business; it's never a bad idea to try or risk something new. You can also source for jobs online, just to add to what you are already doing and also diversify your income. There are different digital data you can take advantage of, in order to discover new areas of revenue expansion.

There are several benefits that come with the diversification of income:

❖ **Maintenance of rising cost:** The rate at which the market cost of almost everything goes up these days is quite alarming, ranging from the price tag on your groceries to your tuition fee. Everything keeps easing beyond one's income by the day. The only way to cope with this increase in price is to have multiple sources of income. Diversifying Your income will not only help you maintain this rising cost, it would also ensure that the cost of living doesn't rise faster than your income.

❖ **Ability to afford huge purchases:** Think about how many times you have had to purchase a car or other expensive things on "loan". One benefit of diversifying your income is the ability to settle these bills and make these payments without adding them to your monthly bills. You can always pay cash for large purchases using your other sources of income. Sometimes, you might be tempted to take out of your retirement fund or emergency fund in order to settle these bills if you depend solely on one source of income. You would save yourself from running into debt by expanding your sources of income.

❖ **Getting rid of job insecurity:** While this might be an obvious benefit, you need to understand that diversifying your income will definitely help you get rid of job insecurity. No matter how promising your job is, you can never tell what's going to happen tomorrow. When something unexpected happens like getting laid off from work, losing a potential client, or suffering any kind of unexpected risk, having something to fall back on would go a long way in helping your present condition. Although, these other income streams might not actually replace your "lost job", they would still help you maintain a normal life when combined with other opportunities/incentives that come with unemployment. The main idea is just to ensure you are doing "more" just in case something unexpected happens.

❖ **Elevating of lifestyle:** One great benefit of diversifying income is the opportunity it gives you to elevate your lifestyle. When you already have multiple streams of income, you might just decide to stop cutting down on your expenses in order to enjoy the benefits you have deprived yourself of. This doesn't mean you have to overspend all because you want to elevate your lifestyle. It doesn't mean you have to follow trends either; this only means you might choose to build a better lifestyle for yourself.

How to develop an investor's mindset?

To become a successful investor, you do not just wake up one morning with a decision to plunge into the stock market without having any knowledge on how to manage risks and how to develop a good attitude towards investing. It takes a very knowledgeable person in this area to take the decision of investing. One thing you have to understand is how crucial the human mind is when it comes to decision making. You are whatever you feed your mind. This is because what distinguishes you as a human being is your mind. Just like your fingerprints, your mind sets you apart from everyone else; this is exactly why two people will never think the same way at the same time or feel the same thing at the same time. To become an investor, especially a successful one, you need to develop the right mindset. It goes beyond psychology; it is simply the nature of humans to fail when they have designed their mind to fail or succeed when they have designed their mind to succeed. Sometimes, we can't help but wonder what goes wrong in our society; it's quite surprising to think that the rich keep getting richer while the poor keep getting poorer. This is only a result of their mentality. Your mindset goes a long way in making or marring you as an individual. How on earth do you expect to manage money efficiently if you can't manage your mind? That being said, here are the five key steps in developing an investor's mindset.

❖ **Get enlightened:** The very first thing you need to do while building an investor's mindset is to get yourself educated. It's quite easy to get swindled in this present world if you decide to invest without doing your research properly. The human mind can be developed through reading. You need to read extensively, take advantage of a lot of information available about investing online and understand exactly what investing entails. If you happen to be someone who doubts other people success stories, it would be a little bit difficult to change your mind, but this change of mind can occur when you get an education about investing and get yourself enlightened.

❖ **Reach out to investors around you:** One other way to develop an investor's mindset is to reach out to people who are successful investors around you. These people would help motivate you as well as provide you with the right information to get you started as an investor. You might also select mentors and follow up with their stories while reaching out to them for motivation as well.

❖ **Be passionate about success:** There are certain people in life who just do not believe in having so much. As long as these people are able to afford their daily meals and put food on their table, they are fine. If you are one of these people, this kind of mindset will only drain every hope of becoming successful from you. In order to be an investor, you need to love money, love the idea of making money, and becoming successful. Of course, you should never get carried away with craving excess money. However, you need to genuinely love the idea of being successful. You need to enjoy the thought of having your money work for you to increase your net worth. This step is really crucial to developing an investor's mindset.

❖ **Watch your circle:** It is not a myth that the kind of people you spend quality time with have a great influence over you. If the people you spend time with happen to be skeptical about investing, there's a tendency that you may never become successful as an investor. This is because their mindset towards being successful will definitely rub off on you in one way or the other. In order to have the right attitude and attitude as an investor, you need to watch the kind of people you socialize with.

❖ **Accept losses:** The last but not the least step to developing an investor's approach is your ability to cope with losses and come to terms with losing as a necessary part of investing. You need to build your mind to accept the fact that investing comes with lots of risks, and coming to terms with this fact will also help you understand that you can minimize risks by investing the right way.

Sometimes we can't help but wonder why people go wrong and never make money. A lot of Americans basically live from pay-check to pay-check and you just never know why. Apart from not having an investor's mindset, there are also other reasons a lot of people will never make money. If they do not break free from these particular attitudes, they might never make it. Although money isn't actually everything and money will never replace happiness in the lives of human beings, we cannot underestimate the importance of money in our day to day lives. Money is a vehicle through which your goals can be achieved and our aim in this book is not to teach you how to make money; the purpose here is to teach you how to remain wealthy and maintain your wealth. Some of the reasons a lot of people never make money are as follows:

❖ **Economic illiteracy:** We have so many graduates out there who graduated with good grades but still find it difficult to make money. This is because academic literacy isn't the same as economic literacy. You could be learned yet remain an economic illiterate. This course isn't taught in schools/ colleges. Your professor would never teach you the pragmatic way to become wealthy. It goes beyond having brilliant entrepreneurial skills. A young man recently paid a huge amount of money just to have lunch with Warren Buffet. A lot of people who do not know how intelligent the billionaire investor is would definitely insult this young man, but little do they know that this man indirectly paid for "knowledge". This is something a lot of us need to know. We need to learn how to boost our finances by understanding how your economy works.

❖ **Comparing your luck:** Until you stop getting comfortable with being broke, you might never enjoy the luxury of success. What do I mean by this? A lot of people find it really easy to say "I'm better than a lot of people". If you keep focusing on you being better than other people, without actually feeling there's a need to notice people who are way better than you, it becomes really difficult to make money. This is one reason why a lot of people never make money. Until this mentality of comparing yourselves with others is abolished, the rich will only keep getting richer and the poor keep getting poorer.

❖ **Not owning up to your responsibilities:** Being dependent on other people for survival make it a little nerve-wracking to make your own money. I personally discovered that being independent actually motivates you to make your own money. As long as there's someone there who constantly gives you money, feed you, and provide you with shelter, you will not feel the need to make your own money. Living with your parents doesn't help you save money; it restricts you from opportunities. Until everyone begins to own up to certain responsibilities, people will always get it wrong when it comes to achieving real success.

❖ **Not getting out of your comfort zone:** I have discovered that I actually work best under pressure. The truth is we all want good things on a platter of gold. However, you need to know that it isn't a cliché to say that good things never come easily. If people would learn how to move out of their comfort zone, it becomes really easy to stay successful.

N.B: The purpose of this chapter is not to put you under any undue pressure to make money or overwork yourself to become successful. The purpose is to let you understand that you can actually achieve real success if you are determined to. The aim is to let you know that millions of people have made it; they achieved success after rising from nothing. You can do it too, if you understood the value of hard work and made good use of it, it would be really easy to make money.

Chapter 2

DIVIDEND STOCKS 101

What are dividends? A dividend is basically a kind of reimbursement made by a firm or organization to its shareholders, usually as dissemination or distribution of profits. A dividend is gotten from the Latin word divindendum (which means to be divided). After an organization earns a taking or profit, the corporation invests the money back into the business (this is known as retained earnings). Afterward, the corporation pays out a proportion of its surplus as a dividend to shareholders.

This payment to the shareholders may be in form of cash which is always deposited into the shareholder's bank account or if the corporation has a dividend reinvestment plan, the amount can be paid by the issue of further shares or share repurchase. This payment is circulated out of a firm's distributable profit. The percent amount to be shared to shareholders is a decision to be made by the board of directors; the board of directors comes together to hold a meeting in order to decide how much the cooperation pays out as "dividends" to shareholders. This decision is then approved by the shareholders.

Sometimes, the dividend is quoted in terms of the dollar quantity each share receives or sometimes, it is measured in terms of a percentage of the existing market price. Dividends can also be defined as a compulsory distribution of income and capital earnings a company realizes, which is paid to mutual fund investors. Different companies decide to pay dividends either yearly, quarterly, monthly, or other times convenient to the company.

One thing that makes dividends attractive to a lot of people is the fact that it is the only income of shareholders and the fact that you get to share out of the profit of a company without being directly involved in the business or selling.

TYPES OF DIVIDENDS

We have several types of dividends:

❖ Cash dividends: This is the most common form of dividends paid by most firms. This type of dividend is paid to the account of the shareholders via electronic funds transfer or a printed paper check. This dividend paid does not belong into the category of an expense; it is otherwise known as a deduction of retained earnings. It is the payment of cash directly to the shareholders. This dividend is paid on the declaration date by the company to the investors who still hold the company's stock on the indicated date. This date on which the dividends are allocated by the board of directors is known as the dividend date of record, while the day the payment of dividends is allotted to shareholders is known as the date of payment.

How does a cash dividend work? Let's assume you own 100 shares of Tianna's company. At the end of the quarter, Tianna's company calculates its financial performance for the quarter. This information is reviewed afterward by the board of directors, along with Tianna's company's profit margin. The board then declares a $0.10 dividend per share for the quarter. This simply means that you are actually eligible to $0.10 × 100 shares= $10.

❖ Stock dividends: This type of dividends is paid out in the form of a supplementary stock of the issuing corporation or a supplementary corporation. A company may decide to share this type of dividend to its shareholders when the company's liquid cash isn't really available. This is also known as scrip dividend and it is sometimes used in place of the cash dividend. A company may decide to give out this type of dividend because it wants to retain its cash for other purposes. The advantage this dividend has is that these stocks are not taxed until they are sold by an investor. How does this dividend work? Note that stock dividends are mostly allotted on the basis of percentage of prevailing holdings of stocks. For instance, let's assume that Tiana's company has made an announcement to allot this dividend of 30 percent. This infers that every individual who is a shareholder of the company will see their stock holding increase by 30 percent. So if you initially had 100 shares of Tianna's company, your share count after receiving your dividends will now be 130 in number.

❖ Property dividend: This particular type of dividend is different from cash and stock dividend. It is a type of dividend where the shareholders are rewarded with assets owned by the company. Such properties include portfolios, equipment or real estate. This kind of dividend is the least common type compared to stock or cash dividends. This type of dividend becomes an option if the company doesn't have sufficient funds to allocate healthy payments. This type of dividend has a financial value even though it is always considered a non-monetary type of dividend. How does a property dividend work? For instance, Company Indigo's board of directors resolves to issue a property dividend for its 10,000 shareholders. The asset circulated by company Indigo is worth $500 to each shareholder. The average market assessment of the assets paid out to shareholders in total is 5 million dollars. The decision to sell or hold onto this asset is then made by each shareholder.

❖ Liquidating dividend: This is the act of distributing cash to shareholders with the intention of shutting down the business organization. This type of dividend is issued out after all creditor and lender obligations have been completely resolved. The dividend payout is always one of the last actions taken before the business folds up.

HOW DO COMPANIES PAY DIVIDENDS?

Companies decide to pay dividends out of their present year's surplus as well as the previous year's profit after regulating depreciation and loss which has been amassed over the years. Dividends are often paid out through the method of a dividend check or the issuance of extra shares of stock. The regular practice for the payment of dividends comes in form of a check which is often sent through a mail few days after the former dividend date, the particular date on which the stock starts trading without the formerly declared date. The issuance of extra shares of stock is sometimes used instead of the use of check by individual companies and mutual funds. One thing you need to know is that dividends are taxed regardless of the form in which they are paid.

DRIP (Dividend reinvestment plan) is really beneficial to investors. If an investor prefers adding to the existing equity he or she holds, with any extra funds from the payment of dividends, automatic reinvestment of dividends reduces to bare bones. This process is contrary to receiving the payment of dividends in cash and then making use of this cash to purchase further shares. Dividend reinvestment plans operated by companies do not require commission since they are far better than using a broker.

Another prospective advantage is that certain companies actually offer investors the alternative to purchase further shares in cash at a certain discount. With a discount from 1-10%, including the bonus advantage of not having to pay commission fees, stockholders can get extra stock holdings at a beneficial price over other investors who procure shares in cash via a brokerage firm.

WHEN DO COMPANIES PAY DIVIDENDS?

The very moment a dividend is announced or declared, the shareholders will be notified through a press release and the information is often reported via important stock quoting services for easy reference. When the dividend is declared, the next thing is to set a record date; this ensures that every shareholder on record on that particular date has a right to be paid their dividends. The day after the record date is called the ex-date or the date which the stock commences trading ex-dividend. This basically means that a purchaser on ex-date is buying shares which are not eligible to receive the most current payment of dividends. The payable date of the dividend often comes a month after the record date.

On this payable date, the funds for payment are usually deposited with the Depository Trust Company (DTC). Afterward, DTC distributes this money to different brokerage firms across the world where the company shares are held by various shareholders. The beneficiary companies appropriately send cash dividends to client accounts or take the decision of processing DRIP transactions, depending on what the client wants. The type of dividend declared and the type of accounts where shares are owned by the shareholders determine the tax implications on the payment of dividends.

HOW TO MAKE MONEY WITH DIVIDEND STOCKS?

One reason a lot of people go into the stock business is for the sole purpose of making money. What do I mean by this? Although a lot of people especially new investors find the idea of investing really impressive, the majority of them do not really know how to make money through dividend stocks. When dealing in stocks, one thing you need to know is the fact that you have to invest in a company that has the tendency to increase its dividends every year. Make sure you look at the dividend history of the company you want to invest in. Make sure it's a company that has set a good record for itself over the past 10-15 years. For instance, if a very healthy and financially stable company gives a dividend of $10 this year, there is a tendency that there would be an increase in the dividends if the company earns more profit in the future. However, the decision to pay or not to pay dividends is vested in the company to make. One other thing you need to know is that your dividends will definitely increase as long as you still hold the stock while your purchase price remains the same. Imagine you purchased 100 stocks of a company at the rate $200. The annual dividend for that year was $10. This means for the very first year, the dividend yield would be 5%. This is a very small yield when compared to the returns from other investments. Nevertheless, let us imagine that this company is profoundly healthy and going to escalate its dividends in the forthcoming years. One other way to make money from dividend stock is to buy at a cheap rate and wait to sell when the market value is relatively high. If you want to make money with dividends, one other thing you should do is to make research and not invest in companies that have a higher debt load than other companies. You can find this information in a company's balance sheet or its annual report. You also need to ensure a company's dividend per share isn't more than at least 80 percent of its earnings per share. Also, ensure the company's current ratio is greater than 1, this certifies the company's financial stability. After calculating your dividend yield, which is the yearly dividend divided by the existing stock price, ensure you spend really less compared to what you earn.

HOW TO CALCULATE A STOCK DIVIDEND YIELD?

What is a dividend yield? The dividend yield is the percentage of your investment that is being paid to you by a stock in the form of dividends. It can also be likened to an interest a stock yields. To find your dividend yield, you have to find the present price per share of the particular stock you are interested in. For publicly-traded companies, the present stock price can be found on websites of any major stock index. Examples are NASDAQ or S&P 500. Note that the share price of any company's stock fluctuates based on the company's activeness. This basically explains why certain estimations for the dividend yield of any company's stock may not be accurate if there is a sudden jolt in the stock's price. The next thing is to find the DPS value of the stock you own. The formula for finding DPS is DPS= D-SD/S. D stands for the amount of the money paid in regular dividends, SD stands for the amount paid in special, one-time dividends, while S stands for the total number of shares of company stock owned by investors. D and SD can be found on the cash flow statement of a company while S can be found on the balance sheet. Dividend yield= Dividend per share/ stock price. If dividend per share equals $1 and stock price equals $20, DY= $1/$20

$$DY= 0.05 = 5\%.$$

The dividends yield here equals 5% in the above equation.

IS A HIGH PAYOUT DIVIDEND GOOD OR BAD?

What is a dividend payout ratio? The dividend payout ratio simply determines the ratio of the entire amount of dividends disbursed to shareholders relative to the net income of the company. It is the percentage of income given out to shareholders in the form of dividends. The company retains the amount of money which is not paid to shareholders to pay off debt or to reinvest in certain important operations. It is sometimes simply referred to as the payout ratio. The dividend payout ratio often specifies how much a company has to return to its shareholders against how much the company decides to reinvest or pay off debts. You can calculate this dividends payout ratio by dividing the dividend per share by the earnings per share or simply the division of dividends by net income. The question now is "how do we know when a company's payout ratio is good or bad?" Companies that do not pay dividends have a payout ratio of 0% as well as companies that are fond of paying out their entire net income as dividends. When a company's payout ratio is over 100% on the other hand, it simply means such company is giving out more than it earns as dividends, which is not really a good sign as such company might be forced to stop paying dividends altogether. When a company's payout ratio is on a steady leap, it may be a good sign that such company is on its verge of maturity and a healthy one to invest in However, when a company's payout ratio takes a huge leap, it could be a warning sign that such company is running into debt or going to end up becoming unsustainable.

PROFITING FOR THE LONG TERM THROUGH COMPOUNDING

In the world of investing, one way to grow your money faster and easier is to invest your earnings along with your initial capital. This act is known as compounding. Here's how the rule of compounding works:

Compound interest will definitely help make an accelerated rate of income when compared to the simple interest which is only calculated on the principal amount. What compound interest also stands for is the fact that you simply earn more money on your interest income which results in an escalating amount of money for you. Albert Einstein once illustrated that the most influential force in the universe was the standard of compounding. In investing, this demonstrates itself through a term known as compound interest.

For better illustration, imagine you have a sum of $500 and earn 10% in interest. This amounts to a total of $550. Now if you earn an interest of 10% on your initial $550, you end up with $605. This continues until you have a very huge sum of money. This is exactly how a lot of people have profited from the theory of compound interest.

This also explains the reason for the achievement of every individual on the Forbes 400 list, and virtually any other human can reap from the amazing benefits of compounding when they invest in the right way. Benjamin Franklin was noted and popular for explaining how the theory of compound interest happens to be the best way to make real money on time. The theory of compound interest is highly convincing and very fast when it comes to making the best of your investments. One beautiful thing everyone should know about the compound interest is the fact that the amount you can save every month is really important. The amount of time you choose to invest in your plan also matters so much. The sooner you learn the act of compounding, the better the knowledge you will have.

Chapter 3

Stock Market Language & Terminologies

Every field has its own "terms" and "language" which have been specially designed and cannot be used outside the field it was originally designed for. Just as the field of law has its own words and terminologies which would never make sense if used in other fields or context, the field of technology also has its own set of words and language. Similarly, the stock market also has its own special language and terminologies. Some of these terms have been compiled in this chapter to help you get familiar with their meanings and how to use such words perfectly. Some of these terminologies are listed below:

❖ **ADVANCED COMPANIES:** An advanced company can be defined as an issuer which is listed on Canada's TSX enterprise exchange who ensures the gratification of the exchange's Tier-one listing criteria. In case you are curious about what Tier one means, it is basically the exchange's primary tier. Only companies with the most substantial and noteworthy financial resources have the right to become members of this tier. These Companies may function in various fields ranging from mining, oil and gas, mixed industry, technology, life sciences, real estate, or investment. The status of Tier-one offers companies entry to a more encouraging supervisory environment, diminished filling requirements, and better prospect for participation by institutional investors. While the purpose of TSX venture exchange is explicitly developing/ unindustrialized companies seeking venture capital, advanced companies have directors who have recognized regulations and the companies in question must have substantial financial assets at their disposal.

* **AGENT:** An agent in authorized terms can be defined as an individual who has been given legal rights to perform certain roles on behalf of another individual or body. An agent may be hired to take the place of a client in negotiations and other transactions with third parties. The agent may be given decision-making authority. Several people use a special agent from time to time. Such agents include a real estate agent, an insurance agent, or travel agents. Two common types of these agents are attorneys who represent their clients in legal affairs and stockbrokers who are appointed by investors to make investment decisions on their behalf. The person who is epitomized by this agent is known as the principal. In finance, it denotes a fiduciary relationship, in which an agent is accredited to implement transactions on behalf of the client. Most people hire agents to perform tasks that they lack the time or expertise to do for themselves. Investors employ stockbrokers to act as middlemen between them and the stock market. More commonly, potential landowners use agents as middlemen, depending on the specialist's greater skills and negotiation. Businesses also hire agents to take their place in a specific venture or negotiation relying on the agents' loftier skills, contacts, or contextual information to seal deals.

* **ALL OR NONE ORDER:** This is an order to purchase or trade a stock that must be implemented in its totality or not implemented at all. AON orders that cannot be implemented instantly often continue being active until they are implemented or annulled. It can also be defined as a command used on a buy or sell order that inculcates the broker to fill the order completely or not at all. For

instance, if there are too few shares to fill the order exclusively, the order is disproved when the market closes. An AON order is considered a duration or an interval order because the trader gives instructions to the broker concerning how the order has to be filled which determines how long the order remains active.

❖ **ARBITRAGE:** This refers to acquiring and vending similar security at the same time in diverse markets to take advantage of a price difference between the two distinct markets. In a market arbitrage trade, an arbitrageur would short-sell the higher priced one. The profit is the range between the two properties. This practice takes its roots firmly in the postulation that an asset that is merchandised worldwide is priced contrarily in various markets. That is, the equivalent stock may have a market value in Europe that is totally different from its value on the New York Stock exchange. In principle, the amounts of the same asset on both exchanges should be one and the same at all times, but market arbitrage opportunities ascend when they are not. Market arbitrage is a careless activity in the sense that traders are solely buying and selling equivalent amounts of the same assets at the same time. This is why arbitrage is often called "reckless profit".

❖ **ASSETS:** An asset is defined as anything which is tangible or a resource of value that can be changed into cash. Assets can be owned by individuals, companies, and governments. For a corporation, an asset might produce revenue or benefit from using or possessing an asset. Examples of these assets include cash and cash equivalents, certificate of deposit, checking and savings accounts, money market accounts, physical cash, and treasury bills. Property or land can also be considered an asset as well as household furnishings, jewelry, vehicles annuities, bonds, the cash value of life insurance policies, mutual funds, etc. An individual's net worth is often calculated when his or her legal responsibility or liabilities are deducted from assets. In other words, your assets are basically all that belongs to you while liabilities are the things you owe.

❖ **ALBERTA SECURITIES COMMISSION:** This is a supervisory organization which manages and imposes securities legislation in the Canadian province of Alberta. Their main purposes are to foster fair and efficient capital markets in Alberta and to protect investors. The ASC, as it is commonly known, is an affiliate of the Canadian Securities Administrators, the charitable canopy organization of Canada's provincial and territorial securities regulators.

❖ **BASIS POINT:** Basis point can be defined as a common unit of quantity for interest rates and other percentages in finance. One basis point is equivalent to one over hundredth of one percent. $1/100^{th}$ of 1% or 0.0001, and can be used to represent the percentage modification in a financial mechanism. The connection between percentage changes and the basis points can be concise as follows: 1% change= 100 basis points and 0.01% = 1 basis point. The basis point originates from the base move amongst two percentages, or the range between two interest rates. Because the fluctuations documented are commonly constricted, and because trivial changes can have massive results, the basis is a segment of a percent. The basis point is universally used for calculating fluctuations in interest rates, equity indices, and the yield of a fixed revenue safety or security. Bonds and loans are often quoted in basis point terms.

❖ **BEAR MARKET:** This is a situation in which securities prices fall 20% or more from topical inflations amid prevalent disapproval and negative investor sentiment. Stereotypically bear markets are connected with debilities in an inclusive market or index like the S&P 500, but singular securities or commodities can be considered to be in a bear market if they go through a decline of 20% or extra over a continuous period of time- commonly a couple of months or more. Bear markets can last for numerous years or just a number of weeks. A profane bear market can actually last anywhere from 10-20 years and is often categorized below average returns on a constant basis. There may be demonstrations surrounding secular bear markets where stocks or indexes rally for a particular time, but the achievements are not sustained and prices relapse to lower levels.

❖ **BEST EFFORTS UNDERWRITING:** This is a prescribed term in which an underwriter gives a promise to make their paramount effort to trade as much of a security contribution (e.g., IPO) as probable. Best-effort agreements are used principally for securities in a less than perfect market circumstance or with advanced risks, such as an unseasoned offering. Best efforts release underwriters from being responsible for any portfolio of shares they are not able to sell. The underwriter does not give a warranty that it will sell the whole IPO issue in a best-efforts settlement. A best-effort contract restricts both the underwriter's risk and the underwriter's earnings since they accept a flat fee for their services.

❖ **BALANCE SHEET:** A balance sheet can be defined as a financial statement that summarizes a company's assets and liabilities plus owner's equity. The balance sheet refers to a specific time. This particular time is typically the end of a quarter, half-year or year. Individuals, establishments, aids, and many other entities make use of balance sheets. The owner's equity basically refers to the shareholders' investment minus the company extractions plus the net income since the company commenced. The balance sheet is otherwise known as the statement of financial position. The owner's equity is also the same as the stockholder's equity or shareholder equity. The balance sheet is one of the foremost financial statement used by accountants. The balance sheet gives an account of what a company's financial position is on a specified date. In fact, a lot of people consider it a snapshot of the firm's financial position at a particular time. Concerned parties such as creditors can perceive what belongs to an entity as well as the liabilities a business has on a specific date. In other words, they recognize what the firm's financial position is at a particular time. A bank uses the statistics in a balance sheet to decide whether to lend a loan aspirant money. The bank might also use it to make decisions about lending a borrower more money. Furthermore, a corporation's management, stakeholders, competitors, and merchants all strive to scrutinize a firm's balance sheet. For instance, before bearing in mind whether to offer credit terms, a supplier needs to be able to tell what exactly the financial stand of the buyer is. Some consumers, Trade unions, and government organizations may also want to know the state of a company's balance sheet. The budgetary aggregate of the whole thing on the left of a balance sheet must be identical to the aggregate on the right. There must be a 'balance'.

❖ **BLACK SCHOLES MARKET:** Black-Scholes is an evaluating approach used to define the reasonable value of hypothetical value for a call or a put alternative based on six variables such as impulsiveness, type of preference, fundamental stock price, time, strike price and risk-free rate. The significance of assumption is more in case of stock market offshoots, and hence appropriate pricing of options eliminates the chance for any arbitrage. There are two essential models for option pricing –Binomial model and the Black-Scholes Model. The model is used to regulate the price of a European Call selection, which fundamentally means that the option can be implemented on the termination date.

❖ **BULL MARKET:** This is the situation of a commercial market of a cluster of securities in which prices are escalating or are anticipated to increase. This term is most often used to refer to the stock market but can be used to refer to anything that is traded, such as bonds, real estates, currencies, and commodities. Because prices of securities rise and fall fundamentally incessantly during trading, the word "bull market" is classically set aside for prolonged periods in which a great quota of security values are escalating. Bull markets are inclined to last for several months or even years. Bull markets are categorized by positivity, investor assurance, and prospects that strong outcomes should linger for an extended period of time. It is challenging to forecast unswervingly when the trends in the market might change. Part of the difficulty is that psychological effects and speculation may sometimes play a huge role in the markets.

❖ **BUSINESS TRUST:** This is a kind of fiduciary relationship whereby a particular party often referred to as the trustor, confers unto another party (the trustee) the right to hold title to certain property or assets for the advantage or benefit of a third party, who is known as the beneficiary.

❖ **BLUE CHIP:** A blue chip can be defined as the stock of a huge perfectly recognized and financially comprehensive company that has functioned for several years. A blue-chip stock usually has a market capitalization in the billions, is commonly the market front-runner, or among the top three corporations in its sector. A blue-chip stock is more often than not a domestic name. Some examples of blue-chip stocks include IBM Corp, Coca-Cola Co., and Boeing Co. While the payment of dividends isn't categorically compulsory for a stock to be considered a blue-chip, majority of blue chips actually have an extensive record of paying steady or rising dividends. The term is assumed to have been derived from poker, where blue chips happen to be the most luxurious chips. A blue-chip stock is, in general, a section of the most trustworthy market indexes or averages such as the DOW JONES Industrial Average, S&P 500, and the Nasdaq 100 in the U.S, the TSX 60 in Canada, or the FTSE index in the U.K.

A company doesn't necessarily need to be big to a certain extent to attain the blue-chip status. A commonly acknowledged yardstick is a market capitalization of $5 billion, while market or sector leaders can be establishments of all dimensions. Although most blue-chip corporations have endured several trials and market cycles, which has led to them being observed as a conducive investment, this doesn't necessarily mean every blue-chip company has the same standard.

❖ **BROKER:** A stockbroker is an expert who implements buy and sell orders for stocks and supplementary securities on behalf of clients. A stockbroker is also the same as a registered representative, investment adviser, or solely broker. A broker is frequently connected with a brokerage firm and takes care of transactions for marketing and institutional customers alike. Stockbrokers often get commissions for the services they render but the individual reward can differ greatly depending on where they work. Brokerage firms and broker-dealers are also sometimes called stockbrokers themselves. Discount brokers happen to be the most sought after and generally referenced stockbroker firms. Ability to purchase and sell stocks and other securities necessitate entrance to one of the key exchanges such as the New York stock exchange (NYSE) or the NASDAQ. To trade on these particular transactions or exchanges, you have to be a member of the exchange or fit into a member firm. Member partnerships and many of the people who work for them are registered as brokers or broker-dealers by FINRA. While you may buy stock shares directly from the business that distributes them, it is more stress-free to

154

work with a stockbroker. Back in the days, getting access to the stock market was far more expensive and as a result, it was only lucrative for great net-worth investors. These investors would stereotypically work with a full-service broker and pay tons of money for implementing a trade. Nevertheless, the upsurge of the internet and successive improvements in technology paved the way for discount brokers to make available less expensive, faster, and more mechanized access to interactions. This has permitted investors to trade the stock markets with smaller transaction fees, making it reasonable to invest and trade unfluctuating with much smaller-sized accounts. So much so that the mainstream of accounts in the market are held with discount brokers.

❖ **BOOK VALUE:** This refers to the entire amount, the value of a corporation would be if it discharged its assets and refunded its entire liabilities. Book value may also represent the worth of a specific asset on the establishment's balance sheet after taking accrued devaluation into account. Book value is calculated by taking a company's fixed assets (which includes land, buildings, computers, etc.) and deducting out insubstantial assets (such as patents) and liabilities – including preferred stock, debt, and accounts payable. The worth you have left after this calculation signifies what the firm is fundamentally worth. Since book value embodies the fundamental net worth of a corporation, it is a very useful tool for investors who want to know if a corporation is understated or exorbitant, which could specify a prospective time to purchase or sell. For instance, value investors hunt for companies dealing in prices at or lower than book value (which specifies a price-book ratio or less than 1.0) which suggests the shares are being traded for less than the company's real value.

❖ **CAPITAL GAIN:** This is an escalation in the worth of a capital asset (investment or real estate) that gives it a sophisticated worth than the purchase price. The profit is not comprehended until the asset is traded. A capital gain may be temporary (a year or less) or long-term (more than a year) and must be requested on income taxes. While capital gains are commonly accompanied with stocks and funds due to their intrinsic price unpredictability, a capital gain can happen in any security that is traded for a price greater than the price it was originally purchased. Realized capital gains actually occur when an asset is sold, which activates a taxable event. Unrealized gains and losses, sometimes referred to as paper gains or losses, replicate an escalation or reduction in investment's value but have not yet prompted a taxable incident.

❖ **CAPITAL STOCK:** The capital stock is the amount of common and chosen shares that a corporation is sanctioned to issue, according to its commercial charter. The quantity acknowledged by the establishment when it gave out shares of its capital stock is recounted in the shareholders' equity segment of the balance sheet. Companies can give out additional capital stock ultimately or buy back shares that are presently owned by shareholders. Capital stock can only be issued or given out by the corporation, and it is the supreme number of shares that can ever be unresolved. It is a means by which a corporation can get capital to develop its business. The stock given can be purchased by investors, who try to find price increase and dividends or substituted for assets, like equipment required for running their business. The exact number of outstanding shares which are shares issued to investors is not automatically equal to the number of available or accredited shares issued by the firm. A corporation can transform this number by voting to rectify its charter which often implies that they want to issue stock to earn or get additional capital.

CAPITAL STOCK= Number of shares issued × per value per share.

❖ **CAPITALIZATION CHANGE:** Capitalization change refers to a variation of a company's capital arrangement which includes both equity and debt. A company's primary capitalization encompasses equity and possibly some debt. When there's a transformation to equity or both modules, (if the debt is part of the capital structure), a capitalization alters results. Generally, a company commences its lifespan with capital donated by the originators, family, and friends. As the company develops, it may look for funds from venture Wealth investors. Any new capital introduced into the company will lead to a capitalization change- basically, a larger quantity of equity at this point. Supposing that this corporation would then be in a situation to search for bank loans or even issue debt. The accumulation of debt to the balance sheet would signify additional capitalization transformation. As the establishment keeps growing into maturity, its funding needs become more refined, calling for several modifications, even alterations depending on the development of the firm and the changing aspects of the industry, to the capital organization. The issuance of innovative shares and supposition of debt for a large achievement, for illustration, could primarily modify the capitalization of a firm. An accountable company endeavors to steady the amount of equity and debt in its capital structure in accordance with its needs. Issuing equity is luxurious and dilutive; debt funding is less expensive and generates tax shields, but too much debt exposes a firm to greater risk. A firm that modifies its capital structure hypothetically must keep the welfare of its shareholders' in mind, but it should lessen the monetary danger to the enterprise. A set of methods of this type of risk is the capitalization of ratio, the amount of debt in the capital structure. The three variants of the capitalization ratio are debt-equity, lasting debt-to-capitalization and entire debt-to- capitalization. What is realistic in terms of the capitalization ratio is determined by the industry and the future predictions for the firm. A company, for example, could have a moderately high ratio unlike its peers, but stronger near-term productivity dimensions to pay down dues to decrease the ratio to a convenient level.

❖ **DISCLOSURE:** In the financial domain, disclosure ultimately refers to the act of letting out all pertinent information on a corporation that may impact investment decision-making. Both optimistic and destructive news, statistics, and other information about its procedures that affect its actions, in a timely manner. Just like disclosure in the law, the idea is that, in the interest of justice, all parties should have equivalent access to a similar set of truths. Although regulation of business had been in existence all along, the federal government-authorized disclosure came into existence in the United States along with the passage of the Securities Act of 1933 together with the Securities Exchange Act of 1934. The two acts were responses to the stock market Crash of 1929 and the succeeding Great Depression. The members of the public and the political candidates alike censured a lack of pellucidity in commercial operations for escalating –if not outright causing- the financial disaster. Since then, supplementary legislation, such as the Sarbanes-Oxley Act of 2002, has prolonged public company disclosure requirements.

❖ **CANADIAN DEPOSITORY FOR SECURITIES LIMITED (CDS):** The Canadian depository for securities limited is Canada's nationwide securities store, clearing and reimbursement hub. It delivers dependable and economical depository, clearing and settlement services to members in Canada's equity, fixed revenue, and currency markets. The duties of this body include the benign custody and association of securities, post-trade dealings dispensation, precise record-keeping and the assortment and circulation of securities entitlements such as dividends and interest payments. CDS is controlled by the securities commission of Ontario and Quebec and the bank of Canada. CDS amalgamated in June 1970, in answer to increasing costs for back-office purposes and improved trading capacities in Canadian Capital markets. It handled roughly 6,000 day-to-day exchange trades in its original year. Today, as a subordinate of TMX Collection, CDS takes care of more than 1.6 million daily national and cross-border securities trades and supervisions over $4 trillion of securities. TMX Collection functions and handles exchanges across asset classes, which includes the Toronto and Montreal exchanges. As the parent corporation has added competencies through procurement, CDS has continued to be the chief benefactor of equities and fixed revenue reimbursement and trade settlement services. CDS provided the trading substructure and technology that permitted the Canadian Capital Markets Association (CCMA) to executive T+2 initiative in 2017 that reduced trade defrayals of investment funds, equities, and bonds from three to two business days.

❖ **CLOSED-END INVESTMENT FUND:** A closed-end fund is a combined investment model founded on issuing a fixed number of shares which are not convertible from the fund. Unlike open funds, new shares in a closed-end fund are not generated by managers to meet ultimatum from stockholders. Instead, the shares can be procured and sold only in the market which is the innovative design of the mutual fund, which precedes open-end mutual funds but compromises the same vigorously achieved pooled investments. Closed-end funds are typically listed on a documented stock exchange and can be accepted and sold on that exchange. The price per share depends solely on the type of market and is frequently unlike the fundamental value or net asset value (NAV) per share of the savings held by the account. The price is said to be at a discount or premium to the NAV when it is below or above the NAV, correspondingly.

❖ **TICKER SYMBOL:** Ticker symbol or stock symbol is a contraction which is often used for the unique identification of widely merchandized shares of a specific stock on a certain stock market. A stock symbol may be a combination of letters and numbers or in form of any of these two. "Ticker symbol" refers to the signs that were written on the ticker tape of a ticker tape appliance. A ticker symbol can also be defined as an organization of characters—typically letters which actually represent specific securities registered on an exchange or otherwise traded publicly. When security is issued by a company to the public marketplace, an available ticker symbol is often selected for its securities that investors and dealers use to manage orders. Every registered security has an exclusive ticker symbol, which facilitates the enormous collection of trade orders that flow through the monetary markets daily. Standard & Poor's (S&P) industrialized the contemporary ticker which is only in the form of letters in the United States to standardize investing. Formerly, a solitary firm could have several ticker symbols among various individual stock markets. The term "ticker" refers to the sound which the tape machines produce, which were one time prevalent in usage but presently have basically been substituted by countless kinds of electronic digital tickers. Individually, the stock market has a constructing agreement which is used for the issuance of tickers precise to that stock market.

❖ **EPS:** Earnings per share (EPS) can be simply defined as a corporation's income divided by the unresolved shares of its shared or common stock. The subsequent number functions as a pointer of a corporation's productivity. It is very common for a business to account EPS that is attuned for unusual items and possible share dilution. The higher a company's EPS, the more lucrative it is considered. The EPS worth is analyzed in the form of the net worth. (It is the same as proceeds or returns) allocated through the obtainable shares. A more advanced calculation regulates the numerator and denominator for shares that could be shaped via alternatives, alterable dues, or permits. You should always consider the numerator if it is familiar for on-going operations.

To determine a business's EPS, the balance sheet and income statement are often used to discover the period-end amount of common shares, dividends paid on preferred stock (if any), and the net income or remunerations. It is more precise to use a subjective regular number of joint shares over the reporting term because the number of shares can alter over time.

Any stock dividends or splits that happen must be replicated in the calculation of the slanted average number of shares unresolved. Several databases abridge the calculation by making use of the number of shares unresolved at the conclusion of an era.

The earnings-per-share metric is one of the most significant variables in shaping a share's price. It is also a key factor used to calculate the price-to-earnings (P/E) valuation ratio, where the E in P/E refers to EPS. By dividing a business's share price by its earnings per share, a stakeholder is able to see the worth of a stock in terms of how much the market is eager to pay for each dollar of earnings. EPS is one of the voluminous indicators you could use to select stocks. If you are interested in understanding, your subsequent step is to select a broker that suits your investment style. Relating EPS in complete terms may not have much significance to investors since regular shareholders do not have straight access to the earnings. As a substitute, stockholders will liken EPS with the share price of the stock to regulate the value of earnings and how investors feel about forthcoming development.

❖ **IPO:** IPO can be defined as a form of public contribution in which shares of a company are sold to institutional investors and regularly also retail (individual) investors; an IPO is recognized by one or more asset banks, who also position for the listing of the shares on single or multiple exchanges of stock. The medium used is colloquially known as floating or going public, a confidentially-held company is converted into a public company. Initial public offerings can be used to nurture new equity capital for the company in concern, to make money from the investments made by private stockholders including pioneers of companies or individual shareholders as well as to facilitate stress-free trading of prevailing holdings or imminent principal raising by transforming into well-known establishments. Subsequently, stocks transacted without restrictions in the open market are identified as the free float. Stock exchanges specify a least free float both in total relations (the entire worth which is regulated by the stock rate increased by the quantity of stocks traded out to the members of the public) also in the form of an amount of the entire share capital (i.e., the number of shares sold to the public divided by the total shares unresolved). Although IPO offers many reimbursements, there are also noteworthy costs involved, chiefly those related with the procedure such as banking and legal fees, as well as the ongoing obligation to reveal vital and sometimes delicate information. Specifics of the projected offering are divulged to prospective procurers in the form of a long document which is referred to as a prospectus. Most corporations assume an IPO with the help of an investment banking firm substituting the capacity of an underwriter. Underwriters are known for providing various services which include helping with appropriately evaluating the worth of shares (share price) and launching a public market for shares (initial sale). Substitute methods such as the Dutch auction have also been discovered and used for numerous IPOs.

❖ **CFD:** CFD is simply an acronym for the term "contract for difference" A contract for difference (CFD) is basically a general form of imitative trading. CFD trading permits you to take risks on the increasing or dwindling prices of fast-moving world-wide monetary markets (or instruments) such as shares, indices, commodities, currencies, and treasuries. The contract for difference (CFD) gives several European traders and investors a chance to profit from price fluctuations without possessing the fundamental asset. It's a comparatively humble security which is calculated by the asset's movement between trade access and departure, totaling only the price alteration without deliberation of the asset's fundamental value. This is proficient through a deal between client and broker and does not apply any stock, forex, commodity, or futures exchange. Trading CFDs give you several major compensations that have augmented the instruments' colossal popularity in the past era. One particular question a lot of people tend to ask about CFD is "How does a CFD Work?" Now, I will give a breakdown of what the CFD looks like. Let's assume a share actually has a standard price of $25.26 when the dealer purchases 100 shares, the charge of the transaction is $2,526 including commission and fees. This trade necessitates at least $1,263 in acceptable or unrestricted currency at an outdated dealer in a 50% border transaction, whereas a CFD agent previously asked for only a 5% border, or $126.30. A CFD transaction will replicate a forfeiture equivalent to the magnitude of the range at the interval of the transaction, therefore, if the spread is 5 cents, there is a need for an increase of 5 cents for the point to hit the breakeven price. You'll realize a 5-cent gain if you retained the stock absolutely but would have been required to pay a commission and acquired a loftier capital expenditure. If the stock marches to an offer or an auction price of $25.76 in a traditional broker account, it can be traded for a $50 increase or $50/$1263=3.95% earnings. However, when the nation-wide exchange reaches this price, the CFD bid price may only be $25.74. The CFD profit will be lesser because the dealer must depart at the bid price and the spread is greater than on the steady market. In this example, the CFD trader earns a projected $48 or $48/$126.30=38% reoccurrence on investment. The CFD broker may also need the trader to purchase at a sophisticated original price, $25.28 for example. Even so, the $46 to $48 earned on the CFD trade represents a net profit, while the $50 profit from possessing the stock outright doesn't consist of commissions or supplementary fees, giving more money to the CFD dealer.

❖ **MUTUAL FUNDS:** What are mutual funds? A mutual fund is a kind of financial instrument which consists of a pool of money gotten from a number of investors to capitalize in securities such as stocks, bonds, money market instruments, and other possessions. Mutual funds are controlled and activated by qualified money managers, who distribute the account's assets and endeavor to produce capital gains or revenue for the fund's stockholders. A mutual fund's assortment is designed and upheld to equal the investment goals stated in its brochure. What a mutual fund does is to help in pooling money from the investing public and use that money to purchase additional securities, typically stocks and bonds. The worth of the mutual fund establishment is influenced by the presentation of the securities it chooses to purchase. Therefore, when you succeed in acquiring a unit or share of a mutual fund, you are purchasing the enactment of its assortment or more specifically, a fragment of the portfolio's worth. Taking the risk to invest in a share of a mutual fund is not the same with investing in shares of stock. Unlike stock, mutual fund shares do not allow its holders any voting privileges. One thing you should understand is, a share of a mutual fund signifies investments in numerous different stocks (or other securities) as an alternative of just one holding. The regular mutual fund holds hundreds of diverse securities, which basically means mutual fund shareholders benefit vital modification at a little price. Take into consideration an investor who purchases only Google stock earlier before the corporation has a bad quarter. He stands a chance of losing a countless deal of value simply because he has laid all his eggs in a basket and also has all his money tied in a firm. On the other hand, an entirely different investor may purchase shares of a mutual fund that happens to possess some Google stock. When Google has a bad quarter, she only throws away a fraction as much because Google is just a minor part of the fund's portfolio. How does a mutual fund Work? A mutual fund is equally an asset and an authentic corporation. This double nature may appear bizarre, but it is in no way different from how a share of AAPL is a depiction of Apple, Inc. When an investor purchases Apple stock, he is purchasing portion ownership of the establishment and its assets. Correspondingly, a mutual fund investor is purchasing part ownership of the mutual fund corporation and its possessions. The dissimilarity is that Apple is concerned with the production of smartphones while mutual fund company specializes in investment making. Investors characteristically make a return from a mutual fund in three ways. Revenue is gotten from dividends on stocks and interests on bonds retained in the fund's collection. A fund reimburses nearly all of the income it gets over the year to pay owners in the system of distribution. Funds usually offer investors an ultimatum either to be given a check for distributions or to plow the earnings and acquire more shares. If the fund trades securities that have augmented in price, the fund takes a capital gain. A lot of these funds also authorize these gains to investors in a distribution. If fund holdings upsurge in price but are not traded by the fund manager, the fund's shares rise in price. You can then trade your mutual fund shares for a turnover in the market. If a mutual fund is interpreted as a cybernetic company, its CEO is the fund manager, occasionally called its asset adviser. The fund manager is employed by a board of directors and is lawfully obliged to work in the best attention of mutual fund shareholders. Most fund managers are also owners of the fund. There are very rare other employees in a mutual fund corporation. The investment adviser or fund manager may hire the service of some other analysts to help with the selection of investments or performance of market investigation. A fund accountant is retained on staff to compute the fund's NAV, the day-to-day worth of the portfolio that regulates if share prices increase or reduce. Mutual funds should also have a compliance officer or two, and perhaps an attorney, to keep up with government principles.

❖ **Equity shares:** Equity shares are the foremost basis of finance of an establishment. They are allotted to the entire members of the general public. Equity shareholders do not relish any superior rights with respect to reimbursement of wealth and dividend. They are eligible to enduring income of the company, but these people have the luxury of controlling the matters of the business and all the shareholders co-operatively are the owners of the company. Equity shares are the shares of joint stock companies which is given out to the members of the public as the core source of durable financing. The only reason it's known as long-term funding is that equity shares are officially not convertible naturally. The worth of equity share is quantified in expressions of the appearance cost of an individual stock, which is otherwise known as the issue worth, respective worth, book value, or market worth. Typically, the asset's value minus liabilities give us the asset's equity value. To curtail this to an equation for bookkeeping purposes, it's Assets-Liabilities=Equity. Equity as a Share of Proprietorship. The term equity has more than one likely meaning, depending on how it's used. For example, in the monetary sense, equity defines how much of an asset each person possesses after all arrears have been funded and liabilities are deducted. Another term used with this kind of financial equity is preference. Preference specifies which shareholders get remunerated first, even if the company files liquidation. Over-all equity shareholders have the benefit of voting privileges, though, and preference shareholders don't get to vote.

❖ **Yield:** This can be defined as the per ratio of a share divided by the price per share. In other words, it can be defined as an establishment's entire yearly-payment of dividends divided by the market capitalization, supposing the number of shares is persistent. It is often conveyed as a percentage.

The dividend yield is used to analyze the receiving on investment (shares) bearing in mind only the proceeds in the form of aggregate dividends acknowledged by the company all through the year.

❖ **What is a Growth Stock:** A growth stock can be defined as a share in a corporation that is predicted to develop at a frequency meaningfully above the usual for the market. These stocks commonly are not known for paying dividends, as the enterprises usually want to plow any earnings in order to hasten growth in the diminutive term. Investors then earn money through revenue allocation when their shares are sold out ultimately. Investment in growth stocks can be unsafe because they do not pay dividends. However, the only chance an investor has to make money on their investment is when they eventually trade their shares. If the company does not do well, investors take a forfeiture on the stock when the time comes to trade it. Today, growth stocks constitute a variety of knowledge, biotech, and some customer unrestricted business. Growth stocks incline to share some little collective traits. For example, growth corporations tend to have exclusive product ranks. They may hold copyrights or access to know-how that put them ahead of others in their business. In order to stay ahead of opponents, they plow profits to improve even newer skills and exclusive rights as a way to safeguard longer term progress. Because of their modernization, they often have a very reliable consumer base or a noteworthy amount of market stake in their business. For instance, an app development corporation that is the first to deliver a new facility may be a growth stock, because it increases market share by being the first company to deliver a new service. If other app corporations arrive in the market with their own varieties of the service, the company that succeeds to entice and hold the principal number of users may become a growth stock. Many small-cap stocks are well thought-out growth stocks. Nevertheless, some superior companies also issue growth stocks.

❖ **SHAREHOLDER**: A shareholder is also known as a **stockholder**; this could be an individual, establishment, organization, or administration that possesses at least one share in a firm. This comprises both corporations listed in a stock exchange and unlisted ones. By holding stocks, a shareholder keeps a percentage of that company. The stockholders are the proprietors of the company – the ones to whom the business is accountable for the business that it does. As well as proprietorship, stockholders have the authority to declare dividends, they can elect who may sit on the board of directors and have a contribution in the business's strategy and purposes. Proprietors of shares in listed companies also have the right to trade their shares at any time they want. Shareholders are not individually accountable for the corporation's responsibilities and amount overdue – the only cash they risk is what they paid when they acquired the shares. This shouldn't be confused with partnerships or sole proprietorships.

Chapter 4

How To Find & Choose A Good Stock

Most new investors are often conflicted in this area. "How do I find and choose a good stock?" This chapter will answer every question you probably have on your mind in this aspect. Ranging from the things to look for in a company you wish to invest in to warning signs you need to study before putting your money in a company. Another important thing you need is the right way to go about diversifying your income while investing. The cliché "do not have all your eggs in one basket" is truly relevant here.

Although there isn't a specific method in selecting and finding a good stock, there are several ways to go about your stock selection but smart investors have their own methods that have paid off over the years. You can also adopt any of these methods as well and might end up becoming an inspiration to several others who are interested in investing as well. Selecting a good stock can be a very difficult thing. However, do not be discouraged, it is an exciting task as well. For me, it is exciting. The process of making your research and trusting your funds with a company with an amazing reputation is an exciting one for me.

In evaluating investments such as stock, investors actually put into consideration the stock's assessment, tactic, policies for modification, and great enthusiasm for risk. Stocks are evaluated in numerous ways, and most of the common evaluating sticks can be found on the internet or in several prints.

The most rudimentary quantity of a stock's value includes what the company pays or what the company actually earns. When you make the move to purchase or acquire a stock, you need to understand that you are buying a part of the company, so productivity is an essential concern. Imagine buying a store. It takes a while deciding on the exact amount you need to spend. Before this happens, you want to find out how much cash that store gets or earns. If the store earns quite a lot of money, you'll have to put in more money to obtain it. Now envisage dividing this store in question into a thousand proprietorship pieces. These pieces are comparable to stock shares, in the sense that you are acquiring a piece of the commercial, rather than the entire company. This explains how stocks are bought and the illustration here is given to make you understand the technical idea in a basic form.

You can be paid by the business for your proprietorship stake in numerous ways. A portion of the profit may be allocated to you by the company, which for shareholders actually comes in the method of a sporadic or periodic dividend. The business can choose to keep expanding the business while plowing money gotten to grow profitability and advance the general worth of the industry. In cases like this, a more prized business makes each piece, or share, of the business more treasured. In such a situation, the more valued share intrinsically worth an advanced price, giving the share's owner capital increase, also known as a rising or escalating stock price.

Like I said earlier, you need to understand that it isn't all companies that pay dividends. As a matter of fact, several fast-growing corporations choose to plow their cash rather than pay out a dividend. Great, securer firms are more probable to pay a dividend than are their lesser, more unpredictable counterparts.

The maximum degree for stocks is the price to earnings ratio, known as the P/E. This ratio which is actually accessible in stock tables takes the share price and splits it by a business's yearly net income. So a stock exchange for $20 and swaggering yearly net income of $2 a share would have a price/earnings ratio, or P/E, of 10. Market experts actually disagree about what establishes a low-priced or luxurious stock. Factually, stocks have averaged a P/E in the mid-teens, though, in topical years, the market P/E has been advanced, often closer to 20. As a universal rule of thumb, stocks with P/Es advanced than the broader market P/E are well-thought-out exclusive, while stocks with a below-market P/E are reflected inexpensive.

But you need to keep in mind that P/E's aren't an impeccable yardstick. A corporation that is lesser and rising fast may have a very high P/E, since it may make pintsize but has a great stock price. If a quality growth rate can actually be permanently maintained, and rapidly grow its incomes, a stock that appears exclusive on a P/E basis can quickly seem like a giveaway. Equally, a corporation may have a low P/E because its stock has been smashed in expectation of meager future income. Thus, what appears to be a really "discounted" stock may be cheap because so many people have come to the conclusion that it's indeed a terrible investment. Such an alluringly low P/E related to a bad business is called a "worth or value trap."

Other general methods comprise the dividend yield, price-to-book and, at times, price-to-sales. These are modest ratios that scrutinize the stock price against the subsequent figure, and these procedures can also be effortlessly found by reviewing stock tables.

Investors pursuing healthier value try to find stocks paying sophisticated yields than the general market, but that's just one deliberation for an investor when determining whether or not to procure a stock. So many people have been really conflicted in this area. The apprehension of "not knowing" what to expect and the fear of being scammed actually put so many people on edge.

Selection of stocks is much like assessing any company you might consider purchasing. After all, when you purchase a stock, you're fundamentally acquiring a stake in a business.

Selecting the accurate firm to invest in may appear to be the first or paramount step in constructing a portfolio, but pecuniary consultants say that an investor who is just starting out, shouldn't essentially "commence" with individual stocks. If you're just beginning to construct your investment assortment, obtaining a single stock is much dangerous and quite unsafe than purchasing a low-cost mutual fund that trails a huge group of stocks, and it's more probable that you'll realize shrill, abrupt changes in the assessment of your investment if you possess just a limited stock.

If you already have an expanded collection of mutual funds and ETFs, then you may want to enhance by including a few individual stocks. With the menace of an individual stock, there's also the chance for better revenues: The S&P 500 increased just 0.75% from 2006 through 2010; in the unchanged five years, there was an upsurge more than 348% on Apple stock. And if you happen to build your portfolio by selecting stocks manually, you'll be able to save some money, unlike an investor who pays a fund manager through the fund's expenditure ratio, to select stocks on his behalf.

Bear in mind that when you're purchasing a stock, you're becoming a share proprietor of that business. So, temporary marketplace activities on the side, the worth of your investment is actually influenced by the health of the business. This simply means that when the company you are investing in is thriving or staggering, the impact is known on your investment. Below is a list of instructions on how to choose a stock:

Buy what you are familiar with. Commence with an industry or a company that's conversant to you; the reason is to save yourself from the apprehension of not knowing what to expect. Other reasons you are advised to go for a company you are familiar with are as follows:

- ❖ **A place to commence:** Everyone actually has a favorite brand; some of us would rather shop a particular brand regardless of how cheap or expensive it is. When you walk into a bar, there is a drink you just wouldn't buy even if you were being paid for buying it. You alone understand why you only shop these products, or how demanding the chain restaurant down the street is on a distinctive night. That's not all the essential information, of course, but it may assist you in putting those corporations' earnings accounts in perspective.

- ❖ **Do away with the flimflam.** During the dot-com fizz, lots of investors fell for stocks without copiously comprehending how those companies intended to make their money. In many circumstances, it turned out, the organization didn't fully comprehend either. What does this tell you? This simply means that you should never consider investing in a company as a result of the hype that comes with it, there are tons of people who have been misled out there, people and the internet could be misleading. All they try to do is paint you a perfect picture with sugar-coating words to make you bring your money to the intended company. Avoid this hype and only consider the future prospect of the company and exactly what the company has to offer.

- ❖ **Put price and assessment into consideration:** Investment experts often seek for stocks that are "low-priced" or "underestimated." Usually, what they mean is that investors are disbursing a comparatively truncated price for each buck the business makes. This is quantified by the stock's price-to-earnings ratio or P/E. (Find that quantity on SmartMoney.com, or analyze it yourself by allotting a business's share price by its net income.) Very approximately speaking, a P/E below about 15 is measured cheap, and a P/E above 20 is considered luxurious. But there's actually more to it than that, it doesn't end here.

- ❖ **Recognize what kind of stock you're talking about.** A corporation that's expected to develop speedily will be more luxurious than a well-known firm that's growing more slowly. Relate a firm's P/E to other corporations in the same trade to see if it's low-priced or more exclusive than its peers. This boils down to the fact that you need to do extensive research while selecting a stock to invest in. Devoting a lot of your time to research would definitely help you make a good decision.

- ❖ **Inexpensive isn't always decent, and luxurious isn't always a bad idea:** At times, a stock is low-priced because its business is developing less or actually decelerating. And occasionally a stock is luxurious because it's extensively anticipated to raise its earnings swiftly in the succeeding years. You want to purchase stocks that you can sensibly anticipate will be worth more later, so look at assessment combined with prospects for upcoming earnings.

- ❖ **Assess pecuniary health.** This is a very crucial step you need to consider while choosing a good stock. A lot of people have made the mistake of investing in an impecunious company; you do not want to make the same mistake as well. Start burrowing into the company's monetary reports. Do a lot of research and take note of every fault you find while doing your research. All unrestricted firms have to announce periodical and yearly reports. You can examine the Investor Dealings section of their web site, or discover certified accounts filed with the SEC on the web. Don't just lay emphasis on the most current report: What you're really considering is a reliable past of success and monetary health, not just one good quarter. Do not risk your money in a staggering company as this might pose a danger on your investment in the future. Putting this into consideration will help you find a really dependable company to invest your money in while choosing a good stock.

❖ **Look out for the company's revenue development:** No one knows what's going to happen on a daily basis, however, in the long run, stock prices upsurge when firms are building and earning more money, which typically commences with increasing revenue. You'll hear forecasters refer to income as the "top line." The revenue growth or increase of a company is a very important thing you need to consider while choosing a stock.

❖ **Find the bottom line as well:** The modification concerning revenue and expenditures is a firm's profit margin. A company that's increasing revenue while adjusting costs will also have increasing margins.

❖ **Know how much dues the corporation has:** It is very essential to know how much debt a company has before investing in it. Find out what the firm's balance sheet looks like before deciding if you would like to partner invest your money in it or not. In general terms, the share price of an establishment with extra liability is likely to be more unpredictable because more of the company's revenue has to go to interest and payment of outstanding dues. You should compare a business to its peers to perceive if it depends solely on borrowing a rare aggregate of money for its business and size. The last thing you want is to be associated with a company that has so much debt on its neck or a company that has a lot of outstanding to pay. If a company falls in this category, you should never consider being a shareowner of such a company.

❖ **Find a dividend.** A dividend which is usually an allocated amount of money given to shareholders on a quarterly basis or annual basis, or a cash disbursement to stock investors, isn't just a foundation of steady revenue; it's a symbol of a business in worthy monetary health. If a business pays a dividend, look at the times past of their payments. Do they have a history of a cumulative dividend or not? If yes, this is a good sign that shows that such a company could be a reliable or trustworthy one.

Things you should never do when selecting a stock

❖ **Don't purchase on price only.** Don't consider a stock that is rock-bottom just because its price has plunged 10%. Always ensure you totally understand the exact reason and how that value is going to recover. When you are sure about this, selecting a stock won't be a difficult task anymore.

❖ **Don't depend entirely on forecaster endorsements:** Specialists' reports can suggest and actually provide some awesome information on the well-being of a company. However, you need to be aware of the fact that they actually turn out biased for 'buy' rankings. But because of that predisposition, a sell evaluation, particularly an innovative sell rating, from a forecaster or analyst can be a warning sign. You need to be on the lookout for some of these so-called analysts.

❖ **Don't be staggered by instability.** There is a ninety percent probability that an individual stock is always going to appear more unstable and unpredictable when compared to a diversified mutual fund. You can examine the 52-week highs and slumps for stocks that you're fascinated with to acquire some perception of how extensively amounts can fluctuate in less than a year or in a year.

❖ **Don't fail to remember to trade.** Definitely, you should have a strategy for how you approach purchasing stocks, but it's just as significant to recognize when to trade. Have a set of standards that will convey to you the exact time to sell: If the corporation scratches its dividend; if the price increases or drops to a definite point; if a forecaster reduces the stock, and so on. Devising a strategy for selling will relieve you from the stress of selling out of anxiety over a temporary move in the market. A strategy for selling can also help you earn your profit.

What are the best platforms for choosing stocks?

Here's a list of online platforms where you can select stocks.

❖ **Ally Invest - Paramount for Inexpensive Trades**

Paramount for low-cost trades

<u>Things you should note</u>

1) Little rates and dues and an amazing user border

2) Pros

3) Rock-bottom rates

4) Stress-free admittance point

5) Cons

6) No prospects interchange

Why you should consider it

1) **Rock-bottom charges**

At $4.95 a piece trade, with virtually no inoperativeness burden and a $50 complete outgoing allocation fee, invests imbursement construction is about as curtailed as you'll realize. Although, a cluster of thoughtless brokers released their directives in 2017 to be viable with Ally Invests $4.95 flat amount. Ally keeps its superiority with a nil account least and alluring mark-down for dynamic investors — fairness trades drop to $3.95 for customers with 30-plus occupations each quarter or a balance of $100,000.

While some mobile platforms like Robin hood boast totally commission-free stocks and ETFs, Ally Invests platform and resources keeps its edge with eminent research and tools, which includes access to its online trader system.

2) Easy entry point

Despite the fact that Ally invest offers attractive pricing, another breath-taking feature it offers is an exemplary platform that affords you unlimited access to the complete world of stocks and ETFs. Where some discount brokers lay emphasis on only one kind of trader (for example, options traders or high-net-worth investors), Ally Invest provides an outstanding knowledge for investors of all kinds. A focus on bargain-basement costs can sometimes be a red flag for excellence, but Ally truly delivers with urbane calculators, profit-loss estimators, and lots more. Ally also offers a healthy exploration library that integrates visual slides and collaborative broadcasting into its market data.

3) Stellar ratings

It is not an overstatement to say that Ally invest offers one of the most remarkable and impeccable services. Barron's has attested to this fact and given   Ally Invests past self, at least four out of five stars for the preceding 10 years, and Ally continues to rack up prestige for its contributions and low commissions from both Barron's and other rating sites like StockBrokers.com.

Points you should cogitate

No prospects trading

1) If you want to trade "prospects" (contracts to purchase or trade assets in the future), Ally Invest isn't an alternative. That's not rare for an online stock broker — neither Robinhood, Vanguard, nor Fidelity bid prospects trading — but you can do it with some other uppermost preferences, as well as E*TRADE, Charles Schwab, Interactive Brokers, and TD Ameritrade.

2) **Robinhood - Great for Starters**

If you are just starting out as an investor, Robinhood is a place to be.

3) Pros

4) Accessible trading policy

5) No directive fees

6) Great beginner-friendly app

7) Cons

8) No bonds, mutual funds, futures, or short-selling

Why you should consider it

Comprehensible trading platform

9) Robinhood is unarguably one of the best online trading platform and a force to reckon with in online business since it was established in the year 2013 by two Stanford alums. Robin-hood revealed their undertaking was inspired by the Occupy Wall Street demonstrations and indicated in the company's name. The

vision is to make investing more reasonably priced and more reachable to millennials. Robin hood's trading interface — both via its mobile app and its website — has turned out to be the most comprehensible of all contenders, which has made it a faultless selection for the first-time dealer. The design is uncluttered, collaborating, and relaxed to pilot. "Robinhood is a worthy fit for innovative investors because it bargains a smooth, modern app that permits you to trade professionally," says a particular stock market analyst and investing and wealth management reporter at Bank rate. "And of course, it's unrestricted with no charge, permitting you to invest money that would have otherwise gone into a broker's pocket."

10) **No commission fees**

Contrary to the laid down procedures of several online trading platforms, Robinhood doesn't charge a commission fee every time you buy or sell stocks, ETFs, or options. If you're a professional trader or a greenhorn without much money to spare, Robinhood is exactly for you. It is an amazing alternative to the $5 to $7 fees per trade presented by opponents. However, Robinhood does rake in "payment for order flow" by negotiating regulatory fees up to the nearest penny and pinching the difference. "That means if you purchase a stock for $100.00, Robinhood gets an amount of 2.6 cents from the market maker," says co-founder and co-CEO Vlad Tenev, whereas "other brokerages receive returns and charge you a per-trade commission fee."

Points you should cogitate

No bonds, mutual funds, futures, or short-selling

11) One disadvantage of Robinhood's plainness is that as of 2019, it only affords you the opportunity to trade stocks, ETFs, and selections on the platform — not

bonds, mutual funds, or futures, and you can't short-sell. But Robinhood is indeed a place for starters and first-time investors. A starter investor will almost certainly want to stick to the fundamentals. If you're fascinated with the idea of bonds and mutual funds, Ally Invest has the best rates. If you want to attempt futures trading, E*TRADE and Charles Schwab are your best bets.

12) E*TRADE – Great for Vigorous Traders

GREAT FOR VIGOROUS TRADERS

Another great accessible platform for energetic traders

13) Pros

14) Volume reductions for recurrent trades

15) Education-heavy platform

16) Low minutest account equilibrium

17) Cons

18) Marginally-advanced commissions

19) **Why you should consider it**

20) **Volume deductions for regular trades**

21) While E*TRADE's starting point fees are a slight high ($6.95 for stocks/ETFs, $6.95 and over 75 cents per deal for selections) associated to Ally Invest, Charles Schwab, and Fidelity, E*TRADE does offer dimensions' mark-downs. If you happen to make more than 30 stock/ETFs trades per quarter, the fee lowers to a very competitive $4.95, and if you trade more than 30 selections per quarter, the

contract fee reduces to 50 cents. That makes E*TRADE a very attractive fit for dynamic traders who keep a handy eye on the market.

22) Education-heavy platform

23) Two things an innovative investor needs from their online stock trading platform are an informal learning curve and lots of opportunities to develop. E*TRADE has both. Its platform brags an archive of instructive videos, articles, and webinars for every type of investor. Once you've grasped the basics, read up on market news, reports, and commentary from E*TRADE analysts. You can also take advantage of one-on-one support: Branch appointments are open to book, and online chat tools and round-the-clock hotline are there to monitor and coach you from wherever in the world.

24) Low minutest account equilibrium

25) E*TRADE does necessitate a stock minimum for first-hand brokerage accounts ($500), which may appear like more than a learner would like to throw in. But that much is needed to experience real development, and compared to the least of traditional brokerages, $500 is an extremely hospitable beginning. Moreover, if you can constrain to a $10,000 deposit, you can get 60 days of commission-free trades.

26) Points you should cogitate

27) Marginally advanced commissions

28) The only real downside to E*TRADE: Commission fees twitch at $6.95. It's not until investors have made more than 30 trades per quarter that the fees reduce to $4.95, which Ally Invest, Charles Schwab, and Fidelity compromise upfront. But

while E*TRADE taxes a sharper charge at this point, there are no additions for cheap stocks or dormancy.

29) Best Platform Design: TD Ameritrade

TD Ameritrade is a dominant, exquisitely-designed platform.

30) Pros

31) Supportive platform for learners

32) Influential platform for experts

33) Cons

34) More lavish than mark-down brokerages

35) Why you should consider it

36) Supportive platform for learners

37) TD Ameritrade propositions two super amazing platforms, specially premeditated for two different kinds of investors. Both platforms are permitted to use by any investor with a TD Ameritrade account. The web-based Trade Designer, though often in the private eye of think or swim, is rationalized and laid-back to use. It will charm beginning investors or anyone who desires an abridged edifying interface. Its tab-based steering lets users flip between trading tools and account synopsis, plus charts, stock screeners, heat maps, and more.

Influential platform for Experts

38) Think-or-swim, on the other hand, is a driving force premeditated for the advanced. This desktop presentation regularly shelves awards for its grander tools

and structures, things any other broker would bill a superior for — research reports, simultaneous data, charts, technical studies. Also included: customizable workspaces, all-encompassing third-party examination, a flourishing trader chat room, and a fully practical mobile app.

39) Think-or-swim is a specific standout in selections trading, with options-trading tabs (just click "spread" if you want a spread and "single order" if you want one leg), plus links that elucidate the plans on the command page. Its Tactic Roller feature allows investors to generate custom enclosed calls and then roll those positions from termination to expiration.

40) **Points you should cogitate**

41) **More lavish than mark-down brokerages**

42) TD Ameritrade has been an influential player in the online stock trading environment for years. The reverse side to such full-bodied platforms? Price. Even though TD Ameritrade dropped its fees in 2017 from $9.99 to $6.95, pretty much every other chief discount broker reduced its prices, too. TD Ameritrade continues to be one of the more luxurious choices out there, even with more than 100 commission-free ETFs. Though its assessing structure is more expensive than those of some of the other discount brokers, there are many traders who think it's a first-class trading platform.

Quality Examination and Tools:

Fidelity

43) Pros

44) Smooth and highly-effective platform

45) First-class research

46) Cons

47) Not all tools are available to all customers

48) **Why you should consider it**

49) **Smooth and highly effective platform**

50) Fidelity's platform wins for comprehensible strategy, with apparatuses to help take the presumption out of discovery funds and prying out policies. Fidelity's platform lets you discover your selections with a smooth and spontaneous design, comprehensive with color-coded positions and graphs that call out what's imperative. You can sort stocks by size, enactment, and even standards like sales development or profit growth. Want to sort ETFs by the segments they emphasize on or their expenditures? Finished. There's even a box to see if you desire to discover only Fidelity's commission-free contributions. A few other discount brokers do offer screeners, but none match Fidelity's complexity and usability.

51) **First-class research**

52) In terms of adequate research, Fidelity is in a confederation of its own. The knowledgeably curious can plunge into research from more than 20 suppliers, which includes Recognia, Ned Davis, and McLean Capital Administration. Fidelity's Learning Centre featured videos are prearranged by topic, but they don't stop after clarifying the notion; they also cover how to relate doctrines to your own Fidelity investments.

53) **Points you should cogitate**

54) **Not all tools are available to all customers**

55) Awkwardly, some of Fidelity's innovative tools are only accessible to high-volume traders: Charting with Recognia necessitates a noteworthy 120 trades per year to use, and its Vigorous Trader Pro necessitates 36 trades per year.

56) **Additional Online Stock Trading Sites to Consider**

57) **Charles Schwab - Great for Proficient Traders**

58) Like Fidelity and Vanguard, Charles Schwab is one of the older brick-and-mortar investment brokers that effectively rationalized its exchange platform for the Internet Age. Charles Schwab still happens to be the best choice for advanced traders who want a full battery of selections (stocks, ETFs, options, bonds, mutual funds, futures) and an extraordinary suite of exploration tools. Best of all, even with all the benefits Charles Schwab offers, it's still one of the lowest-cost trading platforms, with low-priced fees than E*TRADE or TD Ameritrade on most trades.

59) **Vanguard - Pre-eminent for Retirement Investors**

60) Since Vanguard is the principal mutual fund bill payer in the world, it doesn't require a fee for the majority of mutual fund trades. Nevertheless, there are several other kinds of trading which are more luxurious, with $7 per selection and up to $20 per stock/ETF. For that motive, Vanguard isn't a recommended platform for starters or low-volume dealers. Nevertheless, Vanguard is an outstanding option for retirement investors involved in long-term, high-volume incomes, or those considering a place to take their IRA. In fact, Vanguard is one great selection for the finest IRA accounts.

61) Interactive Brokers – Cheapest and affordable Commission Rates

62) When it comes to volume, Interactive Brokers is strictly the prevalent online stock trading platform in the U.S. It also publicizes itself as the "lowest cost broker," and for respectable reason: It only charges a disturbingly low $0.005 per trade on stocks, ETFs, options, bonds, mutual funds, and futures (plus a 7 cent per contract fee for options). Theoretically, that's still complex than Robinhood, but Robinhood only deals in stocks, ETFs, and options. Just as mentioned earlier, Robinhood does scan some money off the top of trades via "fee for order flow").

63) If you're an energetic, high-volume dealer and you want to try your hand in all kinds of assets, Interactive Brokers is a wonderful option, since you can trade just about anything without losing $5 to $7 on every deal. The platform interface isn't nearly as comprehensible as Robinhood's, nor as spontaneous as TD Ameritrade's; nevertheless, if you're the kind of depositor who'd benefit the most from Collaborating Brokers (i.e., an experienced one), you'll know your way around a candlestick diagram definitely.

Chapter 5

MARKET MASTERY

In this chapter, you will get to know exactly how the stock market works and how to efficiently analyze the stock market.

Now that you are already familiar with some of the platforms for buying stocks, the next question on your mind might be how to analyze a stock. Do you happen to be a victim of analysis paralysis? Do you have a stock you are interested in purchasing but you don't have the vaguest idea of where to even begin a suitable analysis? This chapter will answer every question. Sit back and enjoy every detail provided.

Investing in this era is a lot more different from how it was done back in the days, 50, or even 20 years, ago. Back then, you could only get some degree of amount of stock data in the day-to-day newspaper. Now it's quite different as there is a wide range of access to an apparently limitless amount of data on every openly traded stock. Of course, this has its own advantages and downsides as well.

One downside is the fact that there's so much information floating around the web which has made a lot of people get lost in the specifics, only those who know exactly where to look can make more conversant investing choices.

You can essentially conduct a detailed examination of any stock in 12 easy steps: a process known as the Nasdaq Dozen.

Just to put this out there, it is imperative to keep in mind that the Nasdaq Dozen is neither a crystal ball nor a warranty of accomplishment. Reasonably, it is a balanced, repeatable process for investigating the most significant essential and practical aspects of any stock.

It is also essential to keep in mind that no stock is 100 percent perfect. If you look clearly enough, you can continually find a problem with a stock. On the other hand, if you look hard enough, you can always find something worthy about a stock. The point is to put your money in stocks that have better prospects.

For an innovative investor, the stock market can appear to be a lot like legitimate gambling. "Females and gents, place your gambles! Unsystematically select a stock based on gut disposition and water cooler conversation! If the price of your stock increases -- and who knows the exact reason? -- you emerge the winner! If it reduces, you lose it all!" Doesn't it seem like the reason a whole lot of people got rich during the dot-com boom -- and why so many others lost their shirts (and of course their life savings) in the recent slump?

This is not the case. But it's so unfortunate that quite a number of innovative and beginning investors actually feel this way about the stock market - as a temporary investment vehicle that either carries huge financial increases or overwhelming losses. With that assertiveness, the stock market is as dependable a form of investment as a game of roulette. However, if you devote more time to learn about stocks and the more you comprehend the true landscape of stock market investment, the healthier and keener you'll be able to manage your income.

The stock market can be frightening, but a little knowledge of how it works can help ease your terrors. Let's begin with some simple definitions. A **share** of stock is factually a part in the possession of a firm. Purchasing a share gives you an entitlement to a part of the properties and pays of that firm. **Possessions** comprise the whole thing the business possesses (buildings, equipment, trademarks), and **earnings** are all of the money the corporation brings in from trading its merchandises and services.

Why exactly do you think a company would want to allocate or distribute its assets and earnings with the over-all public? Because it's in dire need of money, of course. Corporations only have two ways to make money to cover start-up costs or enlarge the trade: It can either lend money from (a procedure called **debt financing**) or trade stock (also known as **equity financing**).

The drawback of borrowing money is that the business has to refund the loan with a particular amount of interest. By trading stock, on the other hand, the company makes money with almost no strings attached. There is no interest to pay and no obligation to even refund money back at all. Even better, equity financing allocates the risk of doing business amongst a large pool of stockholders. If the business fails, the originators don't lose all of their money; several portion of other individuals' hard-earned money is lost instead.

Possibly the finest way to clarify how stocks and the stock market actually work is to use an illustration. We'll use a theoretical food business to help elucidate the rudimentary principles behind giving out and purchasing stock.

Let's assume that you've always dreamed of opening a cafeteria. You love food so much, and you've done your study to figure out how expensive it is to open a cafeteria, including how much money you could anticipate to make each year in profit. The construction and apparatus would cost $500,000 up front, and annual expenditures (ingredients, employee salaries, utilities) would charge an extra $250,000. With yearly earnings of $325,000, you expect to earn a $75,000 profit every year. Sounds interesting!

The only issue is that you don't have $750,000 (building + equipment + expenses) in cash to cover all of those costs. You could go out to borrow this amount of money, but that accumulates interest. What about looking for investors who would give you money in exchange for a part of the proprietorship of the cafeteria?

This is the rationality that businesses use when they decide to issue stock to private or unrestricted stockholders. They rely on the fact that the business will be lucrative enough that investors will see a good profit. In this instance, if stockholders paid an aggregate of $750,000 for shares in your restaurant, they could expect to make $75,000 per annum. That's a concrete 10 percent profit.

Being the proprietor of the cafeteria, you can fix the original value of the business, as well as the entire number of shares of stock you want to issue to the general public. Fascinatingly, the value of the food business doesn't have to draw parallels with the definite value of the assets or the business's existing productivity. You can fix the amount so that it replicates the forthcoming value of the venture. For instance, if you fix the price at $750,000, investors could assume a 10 percent return. If you fix the price at twice that much, $1,500,000, investors would still get a reputable 5 percent return.

If you dispute a lot of shares, that would bring down the price of each individual share, possibly making the stock more eye-catching to solitary investors. Another deliberation is possession. Each individual who purchases a share of stock fundamentally owns a piece of the company and has a say in how the business is run. We'll discuss more about stockholders. However, the focus now is for you to comprehend that, as the proprietor, you may request to purchase a mainstream of the obtainable shares yourself so that you continue to be in majority control of the business. Now, we will be discussing how to analyze the stock market.

HOW TO ANALYZE THE STOCK MARKET?

Investors rely on stock analysis to find hypothetically lucrative stocks. Common ways to examine stock include technical and fundamental analysis. Several constituents fall under fundamental analysis, which includes investigation of a business's price-to-earnings ratio, earnings per share, book value, and return on even-handedness. Many stockholders also use the endorsements of financial predictors to evaluate a stock. The type of stock analysis you implement is based on individual inclination. Recognize the diverse ways to analyze a stock to find the technique that best turns your monetary goals.

Technical Analysis

The technical analysis essentially looks into the supply and demand of a stock contained by the market. Stockholders who make use of technical analysis believe that a stock's chronological presentation specifies how the stock will perform in the imminent. Little attention is given to the worth of the corporation. The technical analysis places substantial emphasis on the learning of trends, charts, and designs.

P/E Ratio

One of the commonest methods of analyzing a stock is studying its price-to-earnings ratio. You compute the P/E ratio by allotting the stock's market value per share by its earnings per share. To find out the value of a stock, investors compare a stock's P/E ratio to those of its contenders and business standards. Lower P/E ratios are seen as approving by investors.

Earnings Per Share

A company's earnings per share display how professionally its revenue is smooth down to investors. An accumulative EPS is taken as a decent sign by depositors. According to NASDAQ, the advanced a company's EPS, the further the value of your shares, because investors seek to obtain a business's stock when payouts are great.

PEG Ratio

The price-to-earnings development ratio takes the P/E ratio a step forward by considering the development of a business. To calculate the PEG, you divide the P/E ratio by the 12-month growth rate. You estimate the future growth rate by looking at the company's historical development rate. Investors characteristically consider a stock valuable if the PEG is lower than 1.

Book Value

Another technique used to analyze a stock is shaping a firm's price-to-book ratio. Investors characteristically use this technique to discover highly developed companies that are underrated. The procedure for the P/B ratio equals the market price of a corporation's stock divided by its book value of equity. Book value of equity is gotten by misusing the book value of obligations from the book value of possessions. Stockholders consider a low P/B ratio as a red flag that the stock is hypothetically belittled.

Return on Equity

Stockholders use return on equity to regulate how well a corporation yields positive revenues for its stockholders. Analyzing ROE can help you discover businesses that are profit producers. ROE is computed by dividing net income by average shareholders' equity. A continual increase in ROE is a good sign to investors.

Analyst Recommendations

Many investors use analyst endorsements to rapidly examine a stock. Analysts perform a wide-ranging ultimate and practical investigation, and they issue purchase or vend endorsements. Before concluding to purchase or vend shares, investors characteristically use analyst authorizations in combination with a stock analysis method.

What is a Bull Market?

A bull market can be defined as the circumstance of a money market, of a cluster of securities, in which there is an inflation in the value of the market or there is an anticipated increase in the market value. The word bull market is basically used in reference to the stock market but can also be used to refer to anything which is traded. These include bonds, real estate, currencies, and merchandises. Because there is always an increase and fall in the prices of securities unceasingly during trading, the term "bull market" is typically set aside for lengthy periods in which a great portion of security prices are rising. Bull markets tend to last for months or even years.

Comprehending Bull markets

The bull market is actually branded by buoyancy, investor assurance, and prospects that strong results should last for a protracted period of time. It is problematic to forecast reliably when the inclinations in the market might transform. Part of the struggle is that emotional effects and assumption may occasionally play a great role in the market place.

There isn't an exact and worldwide metric used to recognize a bull market. However, conceivably **the most common explanation of a bull market is a condition in which stock prices rise by 20%, typically after a descent of 20% and before a subsequent 20% degeneration.** Since bull markets are tough to forecast, analysts can characteristically only distinguish this sensation after it has happened. A distinguished bull market in topical history was the era between 2003 and 2007. Throughout this time, the S&P 500 amplified by a momentous margin after a preceding decline; as the 2008 monetary crisis took effect, most important deteriorations happened again after the bull market run.

Features of a Bull Market

Bull markets usually take place when the economy is firming up or when it is already robust. They tend to occur in line with the sturdy gross domestic product (GDP) and a reduction in joblessness and will often overlap with a rise in business profits. Investor assurance will also incline to ascent throughout a bull market period. The general demand for stocks will be optimistic, along with the inclusive quality of the market. In accumulation, there will be a broad-spectrum upsurge in the amount of IPO activity throughout bull markets.

Remarkably, some of the dynamics stated above are more effortlessly computable than others. While business incomes and joblessness are measurable, it can be more challenging to measure the over-all tone of market clarification, for illustration. Supply and demand for securities will fluctuate: supply will be feeble while request will be sturdy. Investors will be keen on procuring securities, while few will be eager to trade. In a bull market, investors are more keen to take part in the (stock) market in order to make profits.

Bull vs. Bear Markets

The bear market is the direct opposite of a bull market; the bear market is described by dwindling prices and characteristically masked in cynicism. The usually held belief about the origin of these terms proposes that the use of "bull" and "bear" to label markets comes from the way the wildlife in question attack their adversaries. A bull shoves its horns up into the air, while a bear jabs its paws plunging. These movements are descriptions for the movement of a market. If the inclination of the market is up, it's a bull market. If the trend is down, it is known as a bear market.

Bull and bear markets frequently correspond with the financial cycle, which comprises of four phases: increase, peak, contraction, and trench. The beginning of a bull market is often a principal pointer of financial development. Because public emotion about future economic circumstances pushes stock prices, the market regularly increases even before broader financial measures, such as gross domestic product (GDP) growth, begin to pick up. Similarly, bear markets typically set in before financial reduction takes hold. A look back at a characteristic U.S. slump discloses a dwindling stock market several months ahead of GDP weakening.

How to use the bull market to your advantage?

Stockholders who desire to benefit from a bull market should purchase on time so as to use this period to their advantage. This is a time to purchase stocks at rising prices and trade them when they've touched their crest. Although it is difficult to regulate or know exactly when the extremity and ultimate will occur, most damages will be marginal and are typically impermanent. Below, we'll discover numerous conspicuous policies investors apply during bull market eras. Nevertheless, because it is challenging to evaluate the state of the market as it exists presently, these plans involve at least some degree of peril altogether.

❖ **Purchase and keep**

One of the most rudimentary policies in investing is the process of purchasing a specific security and keeping it, hypothetically to trade it at an advanced date. This approach essentially involves self-reliance on the part of the stockholder: why should you keep a security unless you anticipate its value to rise? For this motive, the buoyancy that comes along with bull markets aids to fuel the technique of purchase and keep.

❖ Augmented Buy and Hold

Augmented buy and hold is a disparity on the up-front buy and hold tactic, and it involves extra risk. The evidence behind the augmented buy and hold tactic is that an investor will endure to add to his or her holdings in a specific security so long as it endures to upsurge in worth. One common method for cumulative holdings suggests that a stockholder will buy a supplementary fixed amount of shares for every escalation in the stock price of a pre-set quantity.

❖ Retracement Additions

This can be defined as a short time where there is a reverse in the entire inclination of a security's worth. Even during a bull market, it's improbable that stock values will only rise. Moderately, it is possible there is a turnout of shorter eras of time in which small dints occur as well, even as the over-all inclination lasts upward. Some stockholders watch for retracements within a bull market and move to purchase in the course of these periods. The philosophy behind this approach is that, presuming that the bull market lingers, the value of the security in question will swiftly move back up, retroactively supplying the investor with a bargain-basement acquisition price.

❖ Full Fluctuate Trading

Conceivably the most belligerent way of endeavoring to take advantage of a bull market is the process known as full swing or fluctuate trading. Investors exploiting this approach will take very vigorous roles: They have to be actively involved in using short-selling and other procedures to try to crush out concentrated gains as changes occur within the framework of a grander bull market. It is important to note that:

❖ A bull market is an era marked by the continuous rise in the prices of assets or security.

❖ The regularly accepted explanation of a bull market is when stock prices rise by 20% after two regressions of 20% each.

❖ Traders hire a diversity of tactics, such as augmented buy and hold and retracement, to make money off bull markets.

A typical example of a bull market.

The most productive bull market in contemporary American history commenced at the end of the recession period in 1982 and resolved during the dotcom bust in 2000. In the course of this profane bull market — a term that symbolizes a bull market enduring many years — the Dow Jones Industrial Average (DJIA) averaged 16.8% yearly revenues. The NASDAQ, a tech-heavy altercation, amplified its worth five-fold between 1995 and 2000, mounting from 1,000 to over 5,000. A long-drawn-out bear market shadowed the 1982-2000 bull market. From 2000 to 2009, the market wriggled to inaugurate equilibrium and supplied mediocre yearly returns of -6.2%. Nevertheless, 2009 saw the twitch of ten-year bull market track. Forecasters believe that the previous bull market started on March 9, 2009, and was principally led by an increase in technology stocks.

HOW TO GET READY FOR THE STOCK MARKET

Stock market bangs or crashes are typically a result of more than one factor. In fact, there are often two sets of causes of a crash. One set of circumstances generates the environment for the sell-off, and additional set of elements prompt the commencement of the sell-off. Just because there is a market fizz, it doesn't mean a crash will occur. Ordinarily, something needs to happen to cause stockholders to commence selling and customers to step away from the typical market.

Extraordinary estimates, dwindling or unsatisfactory business earnings, bankruptcies, dwindling customer expenditure, rising increase, a downturn or motionless economic development, and geopolitical proceedings can all create the environment for an alteration, a crash or a bear market. The commencement of a sell-off is customarily activated by dwindling liquidity.

Falling liquidity may happen if banks stop spreading credit or if a controller intensifies the margin necessities for dealers. Occasionally when a central bank increases interest rates, banks will instigate to call in some of their advances, activating a shortage of liquidity in the market. The humblest clarification is that at some point the money runs out. Markets rise while stockholders continue to purchase, and when they begin to go into debt, markets plummet. The rigorous cause of a crash is often tranquil to recognize in retrospection but difficult to see at the time. So, when will there be a crash in the stock market again? There is no specific answer to this question. The FAANG stocks (Facebook, Apple, Amazon, Netflix, and Google) have commanded the bull market over the preceding 9 years. If these stocks fail to hold onto their income momentum going, investors may lose assurance in the market. So far, only Facebook and Netflix have dissatisfied stockholders, while Apple continues to be a force to reckon with.

The CAPE ratio (which is the same as Shiller P/E ratio) is a long period intermittently attuned amount of equity assessments formulated by the appreciated economist Robert Shiller. The CAPE ratio has been at an archaeologically high position for numerous years, although high estimates alone do not mean a crash is looming. Whether US stock prices today are in a stock fizz or not is arguable. In broad-spectrum, fizzes do not unavoidably imply a crash, except there is a catalyst.

An intensification of the trade war with China and Europe could sooner or later lead to earnings impetus dwindling. Unmaintainable levels of dues in China and other developing markets could also activate a crash. If China's stock market were to crash, that alone possibly would not initiate a bear market around the world.

Nevertheless, if China's economy wavers, it might. Geopolitical uproar concerning North Korea, Iran, Syria, or Russia could also become a facilitator if things worsen enough. It's most likely that the next market crash, whenever it happens, will be the consequence of a perfect blizzard caused by numerous factors. But, since it's not something that can be easily predicted, it's best to deliberate on being equipped for a crash whenever it may take place.

One needs to be very equipped and ready for a stock market crash. For green-horns and beginner investors, it's worth memorizing the following:

❖ In the long run, investors are remunerated for taking on risk. Running away from risks completely means sidestepping returns. Several specialists have foretold a 50% crash every year since 2009. If you had shadowed their counsel, you might have been among the people who lost out on more than 200% of profits just because they were scared of investing as a result of an impending crash which never occurred.

❖ The world's most prominent investors have succeeded in making returns over the long run in spite of several market crashes. They have years that worked out well and of course the opposite. However, they have had more favorable years than less favorable ones.

* There is no solitary resolution that will keep your assets from every bear market. Every crash is altered, and sometimes safe-havens don't turn out to be as harmless as they were hypothetical to be.

* Unavoidably some of the venture choices you make might not end up being the best. This is why every investor is advised to expand their portfolio and not put their eggs in one basket.

In other words, bear markets are part of capitalizing. You can't run away from them altogether. However, you can always ensure you do not get wiped out by a bear market. The Golden Rule is to **diversify**, and occasionally **rebalance** your assortment. When a modification, stock market crash or bear market originates the stocks that drop the most are those that are dealing at the highest evaluations, those with the most dues, and those with the lowest restrictions.

These stocks are referred to as high beta stocks, as they outdo on the way up and drift on the way down. Throughout a bull market, these high beta stocks are frequently the stocks that perform the best. As an outcome, they will mature into the leading positions in your assortment. That's why it's a noble thing to rebalance your assortment and make sure the premium of these *"high beta"* stocks aren't too high. Here are some more ways to organize for a stock market crash:

* Shift to self-justifying asset classes and safe haven investments

* Use stop loss guidelines to make balanced decisions

* Grasp enough cash to take advantage of a stock market crash

Shift to self-justifying asset classes and safe haven investments

To diminish damages during a bear market, you can spread part of your portfolio across the subsequent stock market sectors and other asset classes that are considered defensive:

- ❖ Defensive stocks

- ❖ High-quality dividend stocks and blue-chip stocks

- ❖ Precious metals

- ❖ Bonds

- ❖ Hedge funds

- ❖ Cryptocurrencies

Defensive stocks

Non-cyclical consumer stocks and conveniences trade at lower assessments and typically continue to make proceeds during slumps. These are the businesses that trade goods and services that are disbursed regardless of the economic cycle – narcotics, cleaning products, groceries, and gas are good instances.

High-quality dividend stocks and blue-chip stocks

Concrete yet boring establishments are often ignored and unnoticed in the course of bull markets when stockholders focus on development stocks. When stocks instigate to slither, a flight to eminence will often ensue, causing these stocks to leave behind. It really boils down to keeping the stocks that will endure a downturn.

Precious metals

Several precious metals like silver and gold are extensively well-thought-out as safe-haven assets and have archeologically outdone in the course of most (but not all) market crashes. You can purchase precious metal ETFs, bodily metal, or you can purchase shares in valuable metal manufacturers and excavating companies.

Bonds

Factually, bonds have outdone stocks throughout virtually every stock market crash and bear market. Nevertheless, with bond yields at ancient slumps, they do convey more risk now than they did years back. They are worth contemplation; just be cautious of having too much contact to bonds.

Hedge funds

Hedge funds are a substitute for investors with huge and enormous assortments. Hedge funds use an amalgamation of long and short situations, and other policies to produce returns irrespective of the direction of the general market. However, when bearing in mind hedge funds, you should step with restraint and do a thorough investigation. Some hedge funds have done very great, specifically during bear markets – but numerous others have done very poorly. The fact that it is referred to as a hedge fund doesn't guarantee its good performance during a market crash.

Cryptocurrencies

Though recognition of cryptocurrencies as an investment has been made, a lot of people still consider it a very risky investment. Bitcoins are sometimes considered as a safe-haven just in case of a universal crash due to its regionalized nature, the low connection with the stock markets and the restricted supply. There is no dependable data obtainable on how cryptocurrencies act throughout a stock market crash. Nevertheless, if you're enthusiastic to take the risk, tallying a small fraction of Bitcoin or cryptocurrency stocks to an expanded portfolio could be a meaningful investment choice.

Use stop-loss guidelines to make sensible decisions

If you are worried about how much you could miss on some of your principal positions, you can also consider using stop-loss orders to alleviate potential losses. For each stock, you can fix a few price levels below practical maintenance where you will commence to moderate the extent of the situation. It's advised to ensure this is done long before stock prices begin to plummet so that your choices are balanced and not sentimental. Stop-loss is not normally a tactic used by long-term stockholders. Nevertheless, they can help you cope with the psychological effect that comes with the bear market.

Hold enough cash to benefit from a stock market crash

Feasibly the most appropriate way to hedge your portfolio against a crash is to make sure you always have a vigorous portion of it allocated to cash. The amount you allot to cash is really determined by how much unpredictability you are happy to cope with. More cash means you only lose little. However, you will most likely lose out on revenues in the long run. A lower cash equilibrium will undoubtedly lead to advanced general returns but will also mean sophisticated instability.

One other benefit of holding cash, particularly after an extended bull market, is that you will be able to purchase low-priced stock when a crash does happen. Always keep in mind. after a crash, the peril is much inferior – that's when you want to assign more to stocks, and not as much of two defensive assets, precious metals, bonds and cash.

Conclusion: Formulate a plan for the next stock market crash

As you have been made to understand, preparing for a stock market crash goes far beyond forecast. *"Specialists"* forecast crashes all the time, and most of the time, they might not be right. If you pay attention to all these crash forecasts, you will end up bringing up the rear out on the upside. And nevertheless, you should never be in a situation where your portfolio gets wiped out as a result of the crash. Getting yourself ready for a crash means you ought to diversify your portfolio. You can mitigate the effects of a crash by assigning to defensive and blue-chip stocks, bonds, gold, and cash. Having some currencies in your assortment also lets you buy back into the market at minor levels. The existing stock market is equitably luxurious, but there are no emblems of an impending crash. However, that doesn't mean market circumstances can't alter quickly. That's why you should always be prepared for the "coming" or impending crash.

Chapter 6

DIVERSIFICATION & AVOIDING THE PITFALLS

Since you are the one who is in charge of managing your own portfolio, there is a great need to understand and comprehend how essential diversification is to you as an investor. Although no one prays to encounter a loss, you need to brace up yourself for "not-so-good days". When that happens and you run into a loss, you need other reserves to counterweight the degeneration. Diversification guarantees that by not "putting all your eggs in one basket," you will not be setting yourself up for an unnecessary heartbreak when something goes wrong. Trusting all your finances in the hands of one company might not be too good an idea.

Confused on how to commence?

Many investors diversify by purchasing diverse types of funds. Advisors recommend opening with a broad-based index fund that simply tries to reflect the presentation of the S&P 500. Then you could supplement that index fund with a fund that acquisitions share in foreign corporations; one that comprises of shares of small growth businesses; one that capitalizes in bonds and an additional one that purchases shares in real estate investment trusts (REITs).

There are several websites such as Morningstar where you can discover investigation and information about mutual funds to get you on track. Brokerages will characteristically bargain what is called a "prospectus" of a stock market, and it is important to go through these before creating investment decisions. By expanding your assortment, you'll give yourself a chance to develop your money regardless of the ups and downs that come with capitalizing.

Asset Allocation

Over the years, one of the most common form of diversification is asset allocation. By having rudiments of various investment classes in your assortment—which includes stocks, bonds, cash, real estate, gold, or other merchandises—you can safeguard your portfolio from losing the value that it might if it only controlled one failing asset classification.

When stock prices plummet, for example, bond prices often increase because investors move their money into what is well-thought-out a less perilous venture. So an assortment that comprised shares and bonds would perform differently from one that comprised just shares at the period of a crash. It is also intelligent to expand in the interior of asset sessions. Stockholders who put their money on technology shares in the year 2000 came back crying after there was a market crash and technology stocks hurriedly performed contrarily to their expectations. In like manner, shares remained beaten down in late 2007 and early 2008 as a result of the subprime mortgage crisis.

Also, if it appears unwise to invest all your money in only one segment, this would be exactly the same with a particular stock. That's what many stockholders did in the late 1990s, often as workers of tech corporations who permitted their holdings to become unbalanced in their employer's stock. These fundamentally one-stock assortments were parallel to flagpole sitters in the 1930s, suspended high in the air with only a stretched, narrow pole for sustenance.

Subsequently, in the month of September, they had fallen to underneath six dollars. It didn't mount back until the 12th month in the year 2007.

So the two steps to diversification are to spread your money among various asset categories, then further assign those funds *surrounded by* each category. A smart tactic for individual investors is to diversify via mutual funds. Because mutual funds are groups of stocks, you'll be expanded to a confident degree by definition.

Below are four steps to help you get ready for income diversification.

Step 1: Make sure your assortment has many diverse investments

ETFs & mutual funds

An uncomplicated way to do this is by acquiring ETFs, index funds, or mutual funds. ETFs and mutual funds act as a carrier of different stocks— providing you with instant diversification. They trade inversely, so you'll want to read about each in detail before purchasing them, but they're an outstanding method to expand without getting overly complex.

Index funds

One other great option is the use of index funds; this is because they consist of stocks that reflect a precise index—such as the S&P 500. Your variation may be a little more restricted here, but it's still a sound selection to contemplate.

A suitably-diversified investment portfolio should contain the following:

- ❖ Money

- ❖ Shares

- ❖ Bonds

- ❖ Exchange-traded funds

- ❖ Mutual funds

Step 2: Diversify within separate kinds of investments

Select investments with various rates of returns

This turns out more thought-provoking when you're purchasing individual stocks since you'll want to put in a reasonable amount of money to make the cost of exchange worth it. For instance, you don't want a situation where you have to spend $10 to purchase one share of stock for $200. You should put in a larger chunk, so you save money on fees. As a result of this, several people keep a handful of stocks in their portfolio, which opens them to a lot of risk.

So when investing in stocks, for example, don't quintessence on a single stock or a few stocks but reasonably, diverse stocks in VARIOUS sectors. It's also indispensable to have stocks with mixed-income, development, market capitalization among other metrics. When putting your money in things like bonds, select bonds with different credit qualities, duration, and maturities.

Make Use of Ally Invest

If you're looking to hedge into the stock market, contemplate Ally Invest. This has been mentioned in the previous chapter.

Step 3: You should weigh investments with fluctuating risk

Select investments with numerous rates of profit

In order to diversify your portfolio in the most proper manner, select various investments whose rate of return is different to safeguard considerable improvements for positive investments counterbalance losses in other investments.

Keep in mind, although the purpose is to diminish risk, you aren't constrained to blue-chip stocks only.

Overseas or External stocks

A good procedure to practice here is to look at overseas stocks. Imported stocks from other countries tend to perform a little inversely and characteristically poise out a domestic-heavy investment assortment nicely. You can also look at small-cap or mid-cap stocks, which are undeveloped, and more unpredictable stocks.

Step 4: Reshuffle your assortment frequently

Make Use of Bloom

Unlike the view of so many people, diversification isn't something you do once and abandon. You should reexamine your assortment often and make alterations consequently when the risk level isn't reliable with your monetary goals or approach. I endorse reshuffling your assortment at least twice every year. Or, you could use a provision like Bloom, which is a 401(k) optimization tool which ensures the durability of your 401k.

Employ the service of a robo-advisor

In accumulation, if you find it stressful to keep purchasing stocks and trading them to smoothen out your assortment, you will do well with the service of a robo-advisor such as Betterment, which will mechanically rebalance your collection for you and keep you optimally expanded.

A diversified portfolio should include:

Domestic stocks

Purchasing stocks affords you a prospect to <u>own a fraction of a firm</u> which comes with welfares such as dividend payouts and wealth expansions when the stock upsurges in price over time. Domestic stocks should be a momentous fragment of your investment assortment as long as they bargain great prospects for development in the long-standing.

The world's utmost investor, Warren Buffet demonstrates in detail how to diversify when capitalizing in domestic stocks with his top five stock picks being Apple, Wells Fargo, Kraft Heinz Company, BOA (Bank of America) and Coca-Cola. The stocks signify different corporations in diverse sectors.

Bonds

Bonds actually bid unvarying interest income. They are a smaller amount of unpredictable stocks which makes them a worthy "pillow" during impulsive activities in the stock markets.

Stocks should be a noteworthy quota of a portfolio for an investor absorbed in more on the protection of their investment than development. It is worth observing that bonds don't bid higher yields than stocks in the long term, in maximum cases. Conversely, there are convinced international bonds which provide higher yields.

If you're thinking of going into bonds, you could try this super amazing company called Worthy that's proposing a static 5% yearly interest rate – and respectively, a bond costs just $10. The performance of this company has been really impressive.

Temporary investments

One thing you should not forget to include in your assortment is a list of short-term or temporary certificates of payments as well as money market funds which is very stable and gives you direct access to a list of investments. There are guaranteed insurance Investments such as certificates of deposits are insured/guaranteed by the FDIC making them safer; however, they aren't as liquid as money market funds.

Global stocks

A good mix of universal stocks is endorsed to safeguard your collection against the local stock market "shocks." Stocks allotted by US companies act differently from those issued by non-US businesses since they are exposed to various opportunities from several parts of the world.

Sector funds

Just like the name implies, sector funds can be defined as a type of investment fund which has its focus on explicit sectors/fragments of the economy. Possessing this type of fund and including it in your assortment affords you several genuine investment chances in a lot of economic cycles.

Real estate fund

Owning a real estate fund as a part of your assortment, including real estate investment trusts protects you from hyperinflation. You could also take advantage of the very distinctive opportunities that may not be available elsewhere.

Commodity-focused funds

You can get your portfolio protected against inflation by investing in Equity funds which focus on commodities such as gas, minerals, oil, etc. Investors are also saved from the perils that are connected with commodities since investing in commodities is advised for experienced investors only.

Asset allocation funds

People who are keen and enthusiastic about investing but do not have enough professional ideas and time to develop their own diversified portfolio.

Reasons for income diversification

Diversifying decreases the insecurity of investing

Every financial market comes with a certain degree of uncertainty or insecurity. Investing all you have in stocks can actually mean you stand the risk of losing everything if there is a stock market crash. This is the same as every other investment like the real estate market, commodities markets, currencies, and any other investment. Nevertheless, you need to understand that it is almost impossible for a crash to occur in all the markets at the same time in the same way.

This is the case with assets class investment as well. For example, two stocks of various companies in various sectors experience fluctuations in different manners. When you diversify your income by investing in different investments through different sectors, the prospect of losing a substantial amount of money or your total investment is very low.

Warren Buffet once noted that diversification of your income is "protection against ignorance" making it redundant when you know exactly what you are doing. Nevertheless, Buffet is already a veteran wealthy investor. He has devoted several years and has also become proficient at the game of investing and has equipped himself with several experiences which are far beyond the reach of commonplace investors.

Chapter 7

REINVESTING

What do you understand by a dividend reinvestment plan?

A dividend reinvestment plan (DRIP) can be defined as a program, which gives investors an opportunity to plow their cash dividends into supplementary shares or segmental shares, of the fundamental stock on the dividend payment date. Though this term is often used in reference to any kind of programmed reinvestment procedure organized by brokerage or investment company, it commonly refers to a recognized program presented by a visibly traded company to prevailing stockholders. Close to six hundred and fifty firms and five-hundred closed-end funds presently do so.

Comprehending a Dividend Reinvestment Plan—DRIP

The usual mode of paying dividends to shareholders is either via a check or the depositing of fund into the shareholders' accounts. DRIPs, which are also known as dividend reinvestment programs, allow a shareholder to reinvest the total of a confirmed dividend into supplementary shares, which are purchased straight from the firm. Because shares acquired via a DRIP stereotypically come from the firm's own standby or reserve, they are not expected to be marketable through stock interactions. Shares must be exchanged directly via the company, as well.

Most DRIPs permit investors to acquire shares free of commission or for a minimal fee, and at a momentous reduction to the existing share value. The dollar may be set at a minimum rate. Nevertheless, most do not sanction reinvestments much lesser than $10.

Despite the fact that DRIPs are frequently proposed for obtainable shareholders, some companies do make them accessible to new investors, regularly postulating a least possible procurement amount.

While the reinvested dividends are not essentially gotten by the shareholder, they are always reported as payable income (unless they are kept in a tax-privileged account, like an IRA).

HOW DOES AN INVESTOR BENEFIT FROM DRIPS?

DRIPs give stockholders a means to accrue more shares without necessarily going through the pain of having to pay a certain amount of commission. Although quite a lot of firms actually give shares at a discounted rate via their DRIP from 1% to 10% off the current share price. Between commission free and a discounted rate, the cost foundation for possessing the shares can be considerably subordinate than if the shares were acquired on the public or open market. Fractional shares can also be purchased by investors through DRIPs, therefore, this puts every cent of your money to work. Longstanding, the greatest benefit is the outcome of spontaneous reinvestment on the compounding of revenues. An increase in the price of dividends gives shareholders an opportunity to receive a cumulative amount on every share they possess, which can also obtain a loftier number of shares. Over time, this grows the entire return probability of the investment. Because more shares can be acquired at any time the stock price falls, the enduring possibility for better expansions is amplified.

Benefits of DRIPS to a firm

Companies known for paying dividends actually benefit from DRIPs in several ways. Originally, purchasing a share from a firm in the form of a drip provides the business with more capital.

216

Furthermore, there is a 10 percent probability of stockholders who are active participants in a drip choosing to trade out their shares when there is a decline in the stock market. This is probably because participants have a tendency to be enduring investors who are aware of the role their dividends play in the abiding development of their assortment. One other influence is that DRIP-purchased shares are not as liquefied as shares obtained on the open market—they can only be exchanged via the establishment.

Reinvesting your dividends basically has to do with acquiring extra shares of stock with the money you get. On a lot of trading platforms, it is your choice if you want to do this automatically without being directly involved by merely checking a box. Advocates of this tactic highpoint the statistic that the act of acquiring new shares of a stock that you are aware is a dividend-paying one allows you to grow your investment faster than pocketing your dividends and depending on capital income for wealth generation.

Sometimes, certain programs are provided by firms for programmed dividend reinvestment that allows you to obtain supplementary shares at a discounted rate. One very important advantage of dividend reinvestment lies in its capability to develop your wealth silently, so that when you need to diversify your income, especially post-retirement, you already have a steady stream of investment revenue aside.

I believe you are aware of the fact that dividends are essential because the investor is provided with extra money for the settlement of bills, money to shop your groceries and generally increase your standard of living. You can use the dividends to pay your travel bills, medical bills, or simply have it donated to charity. There's so much you could do with the money. The good news, however, is the fact that leaving this substantial amount of money to accrue for some time, can earn you a whopping amount of money if you choose to reinvest it: that is, use them to purchase even *additional* shares of stock that pay dividends in turn. There are stereotypically two means of reinvesting your dividends, one of which is tilling them back into the firm that paid them (this approach can reduce the risk of liquidation for any one firm but announces more social verdict and give way for blunder in the process); the second means is assembling them together and modifying as if they were new cash just like any other payment. Making a decision to reinvest dividends in a positive industry can actually earn you a better compounding rate and wealth formation.

Reinvesting your dividends can actually make a great difference when observing a single company in separation.

How Does Compound Interest Work?

If you are bent on managing your finances, one of the most essential concepts you need to get familiar with is the concept of "Compound interest". You can use the means of compound interest to increase the return on your savings and investments, but it might also land you in trouble when you have interest compounding on the money you've lent. This basically means Compound interest can be used to your advantage or disadvantage.

The Meaning of Compound Interest

Compounding is indeed an essential means of growing. If you're acquainted with the "snowball effect," then you should understand how a thing can develop itself.

How Does the Concept Work?

One fundamental definition of Compound interest is "interest" gotten on a particular amount of money that was hitherto earned as "interest". This cycle leads to cumulative interest and account balances at an accumulative rate, otherwise referred to as *exponential growth*.

Let's begin with the idea of simple interest: you deposit money, and your bank account credits you with an interest on your initial deposit. For instance, you might deposit $100 for a year at 5 percent, and you get an interest of $5 over the year.

What happens the following year? This is where we bring in the theory of compounding You'll begin to get an interest on your original deposit, *and* you'll receive interest on the interest you just made.

It simply means that you'll earn *more* than $5 the following year because you now have a balance of $105, without having to make an initial deposit, so your earnings will speed up. At numerous banks, particularly online banks, there is compounding on your interests every day and it gets added to your account every month. This makes the movement of the entire process really fast.

You need to understand that borrowing money makes compounding work against you. The interest you have to pay on borrowed money increases your loan balance as time goes on, without having to borrow additional money.

How can you benefit from Compound Interest?

❖ **Save Timely and Regularly:** When multiplying your savings, you need to become friends with time. It takes some time to get enough drive, but that drive *will* definitely accrue and ultimately gain power. In some circumstances, beginning early means there is no need to save as much as somebody who *waits* to commence saving. Even if you abandon saving at some point, your head start can recompense dividends some other time. One thing you need to practice is how to be patient in order to let your money accrue and earn you an enormous amount in the future.

❖ **Check the APY.** Comparing bank products like savings accounts and CDs, you need to examine the annual percentage yield (APY). This considers compounding and also provides a factual yearly rate. Auspiciously, it's easy to discover because banks characteristically broadcast the APY since it's greater than the rate of interest. Endeavor to realize more money on your savings, however, it's almost certainly not worth substituting banks for an additional 0.10 percent except you have an enormously great account balance.

❖ **Rid yourself of Debts as early as possible and Pay More as soon as possible:** Disbursing as little on your dues, as you can may not really help you as a result of the fact that you might hardly make money in the interest charges and there could be an increase in your equilibrium. One mistake you would make as a student who has dues is to stay away from benefitting from interest charges and pay back your interest while it increases in order to avoid getting the shock of your life after valediction. Paying without being obligated to pay will definitely help you reduce your entire interest cost.

❖ **Continue to lend minimum rates: While the interest rate on your dues can actually have an effect on your monthly dues, the growth of your debt can also be regulated** and the period it requires to repay it all. It's challenging to put up with multiplied rates. Examine how sensible it is to amalgamate arrears and ensure your interest rate is lessened as your debt is paid.

You can increase your wealth through the method of Compounding. However, you need to know it isn't magical. In order to benefit from compounding, you need to commence with a particular amount of money, pledge it into an account, and watch your money accrue. To end up with any noteworthy savings, you should do this regularly, monthly and annually. The heavy lifting isn't accomplished by Compounding.

What Makes Compound Interest Dominant?

Repetition of payment actually enables Compounding. Starting out might not really impress you. However, there is an instant change as soon as your interest begins to accrue.

- ❖ **How Repeatedly:** The regularity of compounding is really essential. More recurrent compounding phases, every day, for instance, tend to have more significant outcomes. After deciding to own a savings account, you should especially choose accounts that accrue every day. You might merely comprehend interest expenses included in your account monthly. However, computations can be made every day. Some accounts only calculate interest once-a-month or annually.

- ❖ **How Time-consuming: You can achieve more intensive compounding over extended time.** Additionally, you realize an increased amount of payments to the account when you leave your earnings to accrue.

- ❖ **Supplementary Influences:** The interest rate is also an important influence in your account balance over time. Higher rates mean an account will mature more rapidly. However, sometimes a lot of people experience the situation where compound interest actually overcomes an amplified rate. Particularly, over extended phases, a compounded account and a reduced trifling rate might eventually have an increased equilibrium compared to the use of simple interest.

Compute your analysis to determine what's going to happen and discover the breakeven point.

Your account balance can also be affected by certain extractions and payments, nonetheless, it is entirely different from compounding. Leaving your cash to accrue or frequently tallying fresh credits to your account performs well. When your profit is withdrawn, you diminish the outcome of compounding.

❖ **Compounding isn't affected by how much money is involved.** Whether you commence with a sum of $100 or one million dollars, it actually has an equivalent performance and your equilibrium is exactly the same when you plan the evolution carefully. The incomes appear larger when you begin with a huge payment. However, there is no penalty for beginning little or possessing accounts distinctly. It's pre-eminent to emphasize on *proportions and period* when preparing for future purpose. The amount you make becomes an outcome of your frequency and timeframe.

❖ **Regular compounding,** every day or periodic, actually assists you, however, do not be swayed by the frequency. When there is compounding on your interest every day, you continue to receive more or a reduced amount of the equal APY. For example, an account paying 5 percent APY doesn't pay 5 percent per day. You get 1/365th of 5 percent every day. Still, frequent compounding gives you a little edge to help your money mature more rapidly.

How to Calculate Compound Interest?

Compound interest can be calculated in various means to gain vision into how you can grasp your goals and help you keep accurate outlooks. When calculating, you need to imagine certain scenarios with different figures, and see the outcome if you save a little more or how much interest you would make as time goes on. There are several calculators online as well as financial calculators you could use yourself.

Make use of this formula to find compound interest.

A = P (1 + [r / n]) ^ not

To use this calculation, insert in the following variables:

- ❖ **A: this stands for your amount**

- ❖ **p:** your original deposit, referred to as the *principal*

- ❖ **r:** the yearly *interest rate.*

- ❖ **n:** this stands for the *number of compounding periods* yearly

- ❖ **t:** the amount of *time* that your money accumulates

Chapter 8

ADVANCED INVESTING STRATEGIES

Dogs of the Dow

Dogs of the Dow can be defined as an investment strategy which makes use of the 10-highest dividend–yielding stocks in the Dow Jones Industrial Average (DJIA) annually. Because the Dow is one of the ancient and most extensively charted directories globally — and commonly is seen as a measurement for the comprehensive market — it is not rare for market policymakers to base investing procedures on some apparatuses of the DJIA. The main motive to go with the Dogs is that it offers a direct procedure intended to execute unevenly in line with the Dow.

Dogs of the Dow Procedure

Dogs of the Dow is rooted in the fact that top-class firms do not change their dividend to replicate trading circumstances and, consequently, the dividend is a quota of the ordinary value of the company. In disparity, the stock price does waver during the course of the business progression. This should imply that firms with a great dividend comparative to stock price are near the end of their business phase, so their stock price is expected to upsurge quicker than firms with stumpy dividend yields. In this situation, an investor plowing his money in high-dividend-yielding firms per annum should outdo the general market.

Dividend stocks propose existing income and growth possibility, so no wonder many investors are fascinated with them. All the companies who are members of DJIA are dividend-paying companies who are also among the most important blue-chip businesses in the universal economy. There are several means of obtaining these securities. You can select individual stocks and construct your own collection; invest openly in the Dow via ETFS or instead of putting your money in the whole Dow. You can go with the Dogs of the Dow approach, whose stocks propose healthier yields than the Dow itself. Over and over again, the Dogs have managed to overtake the Dow over the progression of the year.

How Does Dogs of the Dow Approach Work?

The general idea is to make the stock selection an easy process safe process, the concluding one because the world is limited to first-class stocks. As a policy, Dogs of the Dow works this way: After the stock market finishes on the last day of the year, hand-pick the 10-best dividend-yielding stocks in the DJIA. Then, on the initial trading day of the fresh year, invest an equivalent dollar sum in each of them. Keep the portfolio for close to a year, then reapply the procedure at the commencement of each succeeding year.

For most amateurs, though, investing is never as easy as that, specifically with the innumerable approaches out there. So, it befits the regular individual investor to recognize what they are doing with their money. Hence, Dogs of the Dow tools flourish. Just look through the web to see Dogs of the Dow ideas, clarification, scrutinizes, calculators, strategies, forecasts, you could also browse through a Dogs of the Dow website.

DIVIDEND CAPTURE STRATEGY

The dividend capture strategy can be defined as an income-focused stock trading strategy prevalent among day dealers. Unlike other traditional methods, which are concerned with purchasing and keeping constant dividend-paying shares to creäte a fixed income stream, it is an energetic trading plan that necessitates recurrent purchasing and trading of shares, keeping them for only a while–just long enough to seize the dividend paid by the stock. The principal stock could occasionally be held for just a particular day.

Companies pay out dividends per annum or four times a year, but some are remunerated monthly. Traders who make use of dividend capture strategy have a preference for the larger yearly dividend disbursements, as it is usually stress-free to make the strategy lucrative with loftier dividend amounts. Dividend calendars with data on dividend payouts are freely accessible on any number of monetary websites.

Dividend Timeframe

There are four important dates connected with dividend capture strategy.

❖ **Declaration date:** This is the date when the firm announces its dividend. It happens well at the payment upfront.

❖ **Ex-dividend date (or ex-date):** This is the deadline for being qualified to get the dividend payment. There is also a drop in the stock price on this day, in consensus with the declared dividend sum. Traders are advised to obtain the stock preceding this critical day.

❖ **Date of record:** This is the day when the qualified shareholders to be paid dividends are recorded by the firm.

❖ **Pay date:** This is the day when the dividend payment is made.

❖ **Declaration Date:** This is the day dividend payment is announced by the Board of directors.

❖ **Ex-Date (or Ex-Dividend Date):** The security begins trading without the dividend.

❖ **Date of Record:** This is the day dividend is received by Current stockholders on record.

❖ **Pay Date: This is the day the payment of the dividend is issued.**

How the Strategy Works

One very appealing thing about the dividend capture strategy is its straightforwardness—no difficult fundamental analysis or charting is mandatory. Fundamentally, an investor or trader procures shares of the stock before the ex-dividend date and trades the shares on the ex-dividend date or any time afterward. If the share price does plummet after the dividend declaration, the investor may wait until the price springs back to its initial worth. Investors do not have to keep the stock until the pay date comes for the payment of dividend

Hypothetically, the dividend capture strategy doesn't seem to make much sense. If the market is activated with impeccable logic, then the dividend amount would be exactly replicated in the share price pending the ex-dividend date, when the stock price would plummet by accurately the dividend sum. Meanwhile, markets do not function with such accurate precision, it doesn't typically work like that. Most often, a trader gets a considerable portion of the dividend in spite of trading the stock at a slight forfeiture succeeding the ex-dividend date. A distinctive example would be a stock trading at $20 per share, paying a $1 dividend, dropping in price on the ex-date only downcast to $19.50, which allows a trader to realize some net earnings of $0.50, positively capturing half the dividend in return.

CHAPTER 10: DIVIDEND INVESTING TIPS

Putting your money in dividend-paying stock is a calculated means of establishing a dependable income stream and building a passive income. Although investing can be a very risky thing, there is a great possibility of earning massive returns from investing.

It is not difficult to become a successful investor, however, it actually requires a comprehensive knowledge of certain ideologies. Below are some of the things you should consider while investing.

Select Quality instead of Quantity

One of the most imperative deliberations for depositors when selecting investments is the dividend yield. The sophisticated the yield, the healthier the profit, but the statistics can be elusive. If the stock's contemporary payout level is not justifiable over the durable, those market-beating dividends can rapidly dry up. REITs are good instances of how instabilities in the market can openly have emotional impact on dividend payouts.

Choosing an investment that boasts of great stability may imply forfeiting a convinced quantity of yield in the temporary, but the result may be more encouraging, predominantly for investors who have a preference for a buy-and-hold tactic. The income produced by lower-risk dividend stocks may be lesser, but it's possible to be more dependable over time.

❖ Stick with Established Companies: The stock market interchanges in series and it has an inclination of repeating itself every time. When selecting dividend investments, there's no healthier evaluating stick than a stock's previous presentation. Explicitly, stockholders should be directing those companies that have attained a "dividend aristocrat" position.

These are renowned companies that have amplified their dividend disbursements to shareholders unswervingly over the preceding 25 years. Their varieties are easily distinguishable, and they produce a stable flow of cash with an extraordinary possibility of permanently doing so in the future.

Observe the development prospect

While innovative corporations can pay out some remarkable dividends, stockholders shouldn't be making decisions without first conducting thorough research. Apart from observing the previous and current returns, it's also very essential to observe the corporation's impending prospective to intensify its dividend payouts.

This is the principal dissimilarity between growth investing and worth investing. With growth investing, instead of concentrating on what the stock is dealing in presently, you would observe the abiding viewpoint for development to measure how lucrative it would be from a dividend perspective.

Pay attention to the Payout Ratio

The safety of the company's investment is sometimes revealed by its payment ratio. This reveals the amount paid out to investors as well as the amount of income retained by the firm.

If you ever come across a high-yield dividend stock, but the corporation is paying out a significant proportion of its revenue to depositors, that's a red flag that you should be really careful. If the firm were to see its revenue stream abridged, the aggregate of dividends you're getting would go on the chopping block.

Diversify

There's an intensive argument to be made for directing assets on a bit of stocks or leveling a detailed segment of the market. If the businesses or corporation you've zeroed in on have an outstanding track record, that promises well for your forthcoming dividend earnings. Meanwhile, that can be challenging in the course of a market downtown.

One way to diversify your income is to spread assets over several dividend-paying investments, allowing you to reduce risk. When dividends are abridged in a particular area, you might not really feel the loss because your other portfolio keeps performing.

Understand when you need to give up

Investing expert Warren Buffett confidently believes in looking into the future when it comes to investing, but like any keen investor, he knows when to cut his losses. You have to understand the difference between having to wait for an investment to pay off and being there for too long. This can be an easy mistake to make when buying stocks that on the surface appear to be a great value. The problem usually occurs when the company itself tends to fail to deliver regarding growth. You should be able to tell when a stock is going down the drain, but you also need to know when to act on it and when to buckle up.

CONCLUSION

Well, I hope you enjoyed this book and got plenty of value from it to go and kick start your dividend investing portfolio. But remember, with the tactics and methods taught in this book, you can enhance your portfolio with an exponential amount of value. All you need to do is to work on your evaluation and analytical skills in order to decipher companies who offer the best returns while abating risk and diversifying your income.

It's nothing short of a manipulating act, but by obeying the afore-mentioned guidelines, investors may train themselves to become really successful and financially stable for the future.

www.ingramcontent.com/pod-product-compliance
Lightning Source LLC
Chambersburg PA
CBHW051753200326
41597CB00025B/4535